REX BARKS

REX BARKS

DIAGRAMMING SENTENCES
MADE EASY

Phyllis Davenport

First Paper Tiger Printing

Published by
The Paper Tiger, Inc.
722 Upper Cherrytown Rd.
Kerhonkson, NY 12446
(845) 626-5354
www.papertig.com

ISBN: 1-889439-35-5

CONTENTS

Introduction 1
Preface 3
Foreword 5
CHAPTER ONE — PARTS OF SPEECH 7
CHAPTER TWO — DIAGRAMMING BEGINS 12
    2-A. Helping Verbs 13
    2-B. Questions 13
    2-C. Modifiers: Adjectives and Adverbs 14
    2-D. Prepositions and Prepositional Phrases 18
    2-E. Coordinating Conjunctions 22
    2-F. Compound Elements 22
    2-G. Understood "You" 23
    2-H. Direct Address 24
    2-I. Interjections 24
    2-J. Introductory Words 25
CHAPTER THREE — KINDS OF VERBS 28
    3-A. Intransitive Complete Verbs 28
    3-B. Transitive Active Verbs 29
    3-C. Transitive Passive Verbs 32
    3-D. Intransitive Linking Verbs 39
CHAPTER FOUR — DEPENDENT CLAUSES 46
    4-A. Adverb Clauses 48
    4-B. Adjective Clauses 53
    4-C. Noun Clauses 60
CHAPTER FIVE — VERBALS 67
    5-A. Gerunds 67
    5-B. Participles 70
    5-C. Infinitives 76
CHAPTER SIX — ADDITIONAL CONSTRUCTIONS 80
    6-A. Appositives 80
    6-B. Objective Complement 81
    6-C. Adverbial Noun 82
CHAPTER SEVEN — COMPOUND AND COMPLEX SENTENCES 87
CHAPTER EIGHT — MISCELLANY 89
    8-A. About Adjective Clauses 89
    8-B. About Adverb Clauses 90
    8-C. About Pronouns 92
    8-D. About Prepositional Phrases 95
    8-E. About Nouns 97
Challenge 99
Appendix 101
Mystery Challenge 108
Answers 109
Index 151

INTRODUCTION

I began my career as a private teacher for a few families committed to providing their children with a real education. These parents had abandoned a fruitless search for a school in which their children would read the classics of literature, learn the story of history, grasp the fundamental principles of science, and develop the clarity and precision of thought that comes from an understanding of *grammar*.

I knew that a rigorous course in English grammar must include the art of diagramming sentences, but it was no easy task to find a good diagramming textbook in an age when grammar itself is unfashionable. Then, one day, a student's mother brought me a copy of Phyllis Davenport's *Rex Barks*. Here was a masterful presentation of grammar—a well-structured, incremental course in diagramming with clear explanations and memorable illustrations of each new principle—housed in a hand-folded, typewritten book with a stapled binding and a tattered yellow cover. Such is the state of education today.

Schools everywhere have abandoned grammar either as unnecessary or as incompatible with the principles they hold most sacred. Educational theorists insist that the fundamental goal of education is to socialize the child, not to force upon him so rigid and academic a skill as grammar. Prominent linguists tell teachers that grammar is an innate faculty and cannot be taught. The self-esteem movement calls for teachers to encourage and praise, not to correct. The diversity movement grants equality to all forms of speech and rejects the notion of a universal standard. Lending support to the myriad of reasons for expelling grammar from the curriculum is the often-repeated and self-contradictory view, "You don't need grammar; you just have to make yourself understood."

Phyllis Davenport understands that if you want to make yourself understood, you need grammar. Her textbook abounds with examples of the ambiguities that result from an ignorance of grammatical rules. Without knowledge of pronouns and elliptical clauses, you lose the distinction between, "You like Millie better than I" (which means, "You like Millie better than I like Millie"), and "You like Millie better than me" (which means, "You like Millie better than you like me"). This subtle distinction can have profound consequences if you and your wife are engaged in a deep discussion about your relationship with Millie. Or consider the confusion that results from the misplacement of a modifier. To cite a memorable example from *Rex Barks*: "Hanging over the side of the ship, his eye was caught by a piece of rope." (The author wryly comments: "There goes that eye, like a fried egg or one of Dali's watches!") Clarity is impossible without grammar. As Mrs. Davenport points out, "Even the 'educationists' who write books about the unimportance of 'grammar' do so with sentences technically correct."

Even among educators who acknowledge the value of grammar, diagramming has been scorned as an old-fashioned exercise in mental rigor. On the contrary, *Rex Barks* shows us that the value of diagramming lies not primarily in the mental gymnastics it requires, but in its presentation of a systematic method of identifying the relationships among words in a sentence. To any student who has studied this book and is struggling to identify the function of a word, you need only say, "Picture the diagram!"

Diagramming serves another purpose not served by other approaches to sentence analysis. A diagram brings the relationship among the words of a sentence to the perceptual level. Upon completing a diagram, students are given a visual reminder that, for example, the subject and verb are the core of the sentence, that prepositional phrases are modifiers that add clarification to other words in the sentence, and that dependent clauses are subordinate to main clauses. Through the process of diagramming, you both *understand* and *see* the functions of various parts of a sentence.

The art of diagramming sentences provides students with an indispensable foundation for the study of grammar, and *Rex Barks* makes the process of learning this skill manageable and fun. The book is laid out in logical, incremental steps, and students are given the opportunity to master one concept before proceeding to the next. They begin with sentences like "Rex barks," and work their way up through modifiers, prepositions, verbs, clauses, verbals, and other complexities of grammar, until, to their delight, they are able to diagram the first sentence in the U.S. Constitution.

One of the best features of *Rex Barks* is the ever-present personality of the author. Mrs. Davenport reminds the reader of that teacher we all once knew: the strict, demanding teacher who made her students think and work hard, who knew her subject and required that her students learn it, who never accepted excuses— and who was loved best by everyone in the school. The book is filled with her firm admonitions for students to stay in focus. (In response to the question of how one can ever learn the difficult task of distinguishing among the various types of verbs, she says, "By THINKING.") It contains many clever devices to help students with tricky concepts (e.g., prepositions are to be remembered as "anything a squirrel can do to a tree.") And it is pervaded by her sense of humor and enthusiasm for her subject.

I am delighted that The Paper Tiger is republishing this gem of grammar instruction. If today's schools awaken to the importance of grammar, *Rex Barks* will be available to help them teach their students the lost art of diagramming. Such, I hope, will be the state of education tomorrow.

Lisa VanDamme
Director, VanDamme Academy
Laguna Hills, CA
December 2003

PREFACE

When I published this book in 1976, I ordered 500 copies. I wanted to use them with my high school English classes, and I hoped I could sell the rest. Soon the 500 were nearly gone, so I had 1000 more printed. These lasted so many years that I felt like Thoreau commenting on his library of 1000 books—hundreds of which, he wryly admitted, he had written himself.

Recently the last little stack was snatched up by a local network of home-schoolers. While REX BARKS had not become the cult book of my fantasies, I began to hope again.

In the years since I wrote *Rex,* the education establishment has seemed to me to have become even less friendly to disciplined, orderly learning of skills and knowledge: The brain chip in children's heads that used to be programmed with multiplication tables has only rap lyrics on it now, and precision in language, if it is acquired, must be caught, rather than taught, by those who read widely in unrequired volumes. Most people will never be sure why "with Joe and I" is wrong, or even that it is.

I have read that diagramming is taught in the private school our President's daughter attended; other little bands in elite settings are probably quietly gathering this knowledge. Here it is for you.

Phyllis Davenport
1999

FOREWORD

If you have opened this book and are reading these words, I hope it is because you find language deeply interesting.

If you are a word-puzzle fan, or if you like logical solutions to problems—mysteries solved with no loose ends—then diagramming will be fun for you.

Of course, you may be faced with the problem of passing an English course which requires you to understand such things as objects and modifiers and participles. In that case, whether or not you find this book exciting, you will be helped by it.

A friend asked me, "How can you write a whole book about diagramming sentences?"

I needed a "whole book" about it.

For diagramming has been in the shadows. If you find a grammar text that deals with diagramming at all, it will do so in two or three almost apologetic pages. I didn't learn it that way. Nor did I learn it from a book. Step by step, Miss Chalfant drilled it into me. I don't know where she learned it.

Now it seems that people are talking about diagramming sentences again. Or talking about NOT diagramming them. They are wondering where it went. Well, one place it went was into my head, thanks to Miss C., and through the years I have taught it to anyone who would listen (and to many more who would not). Often I have been asked, "Why isn't all this in a book?"

So now it is. I hope it will give you value and pleasure. Naturally, what you harvest will depend on your labor.

You will also need to look at things in a new way, and we shall begin with the most important of such things, the SENTENCE.

THE SENTENCE

Did you ever stop to ask yourself, "What is a sentence?" Or did you just memorize the definition the teacher gave: "A sentence is a group of words expressing a complete thought." (That's what Miss Wible taught me.) Some definitions include the phrase, "with a subject and verb."

The more I have thought about a sentence, the less I have been satisfied by that definition. Why do we have sentences, anyway? My guess is that the sentence is the only way we can express the things we want to communicate. What do we want to tell? Or find out? We are interested when

SOMEBODY OR SOMETHING	DOES OR IS SOMETHING

That is my definition of a sentence. Here are some illustrations:

A.

Harry	stole the cheese.

(Harry did something.)

B.

The dog	was so hungry that he ate my shoes.

(The dog was something: very hungry.)

C.

Somebody	broke the window.

(We want to know who did the action.)

D.

Norman	did it.

(Now we know.)

WHY STUDY THE SENTENCE? We all speak them naturally, so why study how a sentence is constructed? There are many reasons.

1. Power continues to be, generally, in the hands of the educated, who notice when a sentence has something dreadfully wrong with it. Even the "educationists" who write books about the unimportance of "grammar" do so with sentences technically correct.

2. Much poetic writing cannot be understood, and therefore cannot be enjoyed, without the skill of turning around unusual word order, "finding the subject and the verb."

3. The study of foreign languages is heavy work without the knowledge of how a sentence operates.

4. Finally, it is satisfying to understand something. You know this. Whether your skill is rebuilding a carburetor or programming a VCR, or getting a grilled cheese sandwich toasty but not burned, you have surely tasted the pleasure of competence. Knowledge can bring joy!

WHAT IS DIAGRAMMING, ANYWAY? Diagramming is a form of sentence analysis which requires one to take the sentence apart and show the relationship of EACH WORD to the rest of the sentence. A sentence diagram is like a puzzle which is not solved until all the parts are in the right place, and none are left over.

You may think of diagramming as a kind of dissection; as each part is taken out, it is identified and its relationship to the rest of the whole is revealed. And, of course, when you are finished with the sentence, you can put it back together more successfully than you can a dissected frog!

And so, let us get to work. Each section of this book will give you some new steps to learn. Work on the practice exercises after you have studied each step, check your answers, and move along to the next level.

CAUTION: STAY AWAKE! SLEEP-LEARNING WON'T WORK! (Thousands of my students have proved this.)

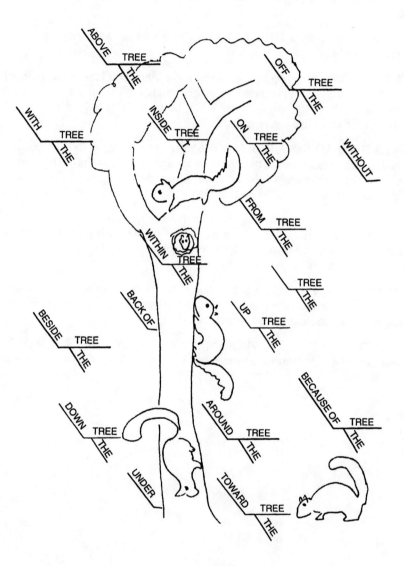

A preposition
is
"anything a squirrel can do to a tree"

CHAPTER ONE
PARTS OF SPEECH

Every word in a sentence does some job. A WORD'S PART OF SPEECH IS THE JOB IT DOES IN ITS SENTENCE.

Every word in a sentence is doing one of eight jobs. We cannot be sure what part of speech a word is until we see what it is doing in its sentence.

You may already know the parts of speech. Check the first part of the APPENDIX of this book for a quick overview of them. If you have never learned them before, you must absolutely do so now. Go over each one until you thoroughly understand it. Try to think up examples of each kind. Check the dictionary to see if you got them right. Progress in learning about sentence structure is YOUR RESPONSIBILITY. It starts here.

1. NOUN—A noun names a person, place, thing, or idea.

Find the NOUNS in this sentence:

Bill called me "Cutie," so I gave him a valentine with candy in it.

(You should have found two persons and two things.)

Full of ambition, she attended college in the nearest city, Forestville.

(You should have found an idea and three places.)

Answers: Bill, Cutie, valentine, candy, ambition, college, city, Forestville.

Bill, Cutie, and Forestville are "proper" nouns—they start with capital letters. The rest are "common" nouns—they are not capitalized.

There is only one "abstract" noun, "ambition." It is an idea that you can't perceive with the senses. The rest are "concrete nouns."
"Me," "I," and "him" DO refer to people, but since they take the place of "Bill" and "Cutie," they are pronouns. "She" is also a pronoun, but we don't know its antecedent (the name or word a pronoun refers to.)

While the basic NOUN JOB is naming things, NOUNS will be subdivided into quite a few categories. They will still NAME things, but they will have various functions in the sentence: SUBJECTS, OBJECTS, APPOSITIVES, etc. Don't let this frighten you. IF IT'S A NAME, IT'S A NOUN in some capacity, even being adjectives and adverbs! (You'll see this later).

Exercise 1-1: Write down all the nouns you can find in these sentences. Then check with the answers in the back of the book.

1. The lean black cat sat on the rusty fence singing to the Siamese in the window.
2. Rex, who had chewed up the slipper, licked father with his tongue.
3. My birthday, next Tuesday, will be celebrated in peace and quiet, since all my friends have gone on vacation.
4. Medicine Hat, Nebraska, is far from Boston; its culture is somewhat different, but it is home to Harry.

Perhaps you have heard "the" called a "determiner." This means that when you see "the," you can expect a noun to follow. It may follow immediately: the wolf. Or there may be adjectives before the noun: the big bad wolf.

2. PRONOUN—A pronoun takes the place of a noun.

You are familiar with PERSONAL pronouns—I, you, he, etc.—that take the place of names of people. Other pronouns stand for indefinite quantities or unknown persons - some, someone, any, etc. You will learn more about some pronouns in this book, but we will not cover all of them. If you find a word DOING A NOUN JOB but NOT definitely naming a person, place, thing, or quality, you probably have a pronoun.

Exercise 1-2: See how many pronouns you can find in these sentences and then check with the answers.

1. He told me who took my pencil, but it was too late to get it back.
2. Somebody wrote something on the board, but no one can read it.
3. Who can say whether this will be a good plan for us?
4. Those are Brussels sprouts; can you tell what these are?
5. The boy whose name I have forgotten left before I paid him everything I owed him.

3. VERB—A verb is a word of action or being.

Chapter 3 will tell you more about verbs than you want to know. Right now make sure you can pick out the word of action: run; dance; rain; skip; destroy; sleep; vegetate; economize; think. You can see that some actions are mental actions, some are very inactive actions. Then get to know the HELPING VERBS that go ahead of the words of action sometimes:

MAY CAN MUST MIGHT SHALL WILL SHOULD WOULD COULD HAVE DO BE

Examples: <u>Has</u> run, <u>did</u> dance, <u>might</u> rain, <u>could have been</u> skipping, <u>will be</u> destroyed, <u>must have</u> slept, <u>shall</u> vegetate, <u>can</u> economize, <u>may have been</u> thinking.

The verbs of being are what we call "linking verbs." You will study those later. The most important is the verb "to be," which comes in these forms, or "parts":
AM ARE IS WAS WERE BEING BEEN
These verbs of being can have helpers:
<u>shall have</u> been, <u>was</u> being, <u>might</u> be

Exercise 1-3: Write all the complete verbs—that means include all helpers. There may be more than one verb per sentence.

1. Laura and Nancy competed for Jeff's attention, but he was interested only in Gail.
2. Because he has been coming to your house so often, your grocery bill has increased dramatically.
3. Rex might have been the dog who upset your trash that you had left on your sidewalk.
4. It has really been snowing since the sun went down.

4. ADJECTIVE—An adjective modifies a noun or pronoun.

What can we know about a certain noun (or pronoun)? Take, for example, BOX. We can know:

WHICH ONE?	THAT	box
WHAT KIND?	WOODEN	box
WHOSE?	RALPH'S	box
HOW MANY?	THREE	boxes

The words which answer these questions about nouns are ADJECTIVES.

Exercise 1-4: Find the adjectives. Include the "articles," <u>a</u>, <u>an</u>, and <u>the</u>.

1. Three fat blackbirds with red patches on their wings sat on our telephone wire.
2. The only way to make a really good sundae is to include chocolate, vanilla, and strawberry ice cream, maple syrup, chopped nuts, and marshmallow sauce.
3. After an enormous Sunday dinner, the old farmer walked slowly to the vine-covered porch and eased into the creaking swing to begin his regular Sunday nap.

5. ADVERB—An adverb modifies a verb, adjective, or other adverb.

What can we know about a certain verb (or adjective or adverb), for example, "HAD RUN"? We can know:
WHEN?   had run YESTERDAY

WHERE?   had run AWAY
WHY?   (this is hard to do in one word)
HOW?   had run QUICKLY

Here are examples of ADVERBS modifying ADJECTIVES:
a VERY big tree (HOW big?)   TOO easy   REALLY serious

Here are examples of ADVERBS modifying OTHER ADVERBS:
VERY quickly   NEVER again (WHEN again?)   QUITE slowly
SO hungrily

Exercise 1-5: Find the adverbs.

1. Suddenly the sky became very dark, the wind blew wildly, and the rain hurriedly began.
2. When the ingredients are thoroughly mixed, very carefully pour the mixture into the well-greased pans.
3. She stared gloomily out the window, fully convinced that the snow would not begin soon enough.
4. I will never tell you a secret again, for you betrayed my trust so very eagerly!

6. CONJUNCTION—A conjunction joins two words, phrases, or clauses.

There are two kinds of CONJUNCTIONS.

COORDINATING conjunction—joins **EQUALS**
SUBORDINATING conjunction—joins **DEPENDENT** clause to
                                      INDEPENDENT clause

<u>CO</u>ordinating conjunctions are: AND BUT OR NOR FOR

Examples: Love AND marriage; cake OR pie; He came BUT I went; He did not speak, NOR did I; I spoke, FOR he couldn't.

<u>SUB</u>ordinating conjunctions include such words as: whenever; since; because; until; if.

Examples: We cried BECAUSE we were sad.   SINCE it rained, we stayed home.   AFTER he spoke, the room was quiet.

NOTE: There is another group of words called CONJUNCTIVE ADVERBS. They are regarded as ADVERBS.
Examples: I think; THEREFORE, I am.   We are tired, YET he stays. The window is open; NEVERTHELESS, it is hot in here.

7. PREPOSITION—A preposition connects a noun or pronoun to the rest of the sentence, showing some relationship.

Chapter 2 will examine prepositions and prepositional phrases in detail. Meanwhile, see how well you can recall (or learn) how to spot a prepositional phrase. PREPOSITIONS ALWAYS OCCUR IN PREPOSITIONAL PHRASES: THERE WILL ALWAYS BE AN OBJECT (A NOUN OR PRONOUN) OF EVERY PREPOSITION.

Example: He glanced into the box. "Into" is the preposition; "box" is the object.

Examine these PREPOSITIONAL PHRASES:

He searched behind the couch, under the table, above the mantel, on the porch, in the cellar, and beneath the laundry.

Exercise 1-6: Find the prepositional phrases. Note that the object may be delayed by one or more ADJECTIVES after the preposition.

1. In spring we look eagerly for signs of new life in our yard.
2. After school Jay ran to the store, eager for a way to spend the dollar he got for his birthday.
3. During this terrible, suffocating heat wave, even the stores have closed, since no one ventures out of his house.
4. To his credit he told the truth about the robbery.
5. I know that in the dark of the night, things look bigger to children, and I remember the lion under my bed.

8. INTERJECTION—An interjection expresses emotion. It is not connected grammatically to the sentence.

Examples: Wow! Look at that!   Oh! I forgot my keys!   Alas, it is too late.
Hooray! We won!

CHAPTER TWO
DIAGRAMMING BEGINS

Get a small straight-edge, a pencil with plenty of eraser, and enough paper so that you can spread out your work comfortably. Here is your first diagram done for you:

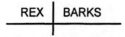

Every sentence MUST have a subject and verb. The subject will be some kind of noun; the verb will be some word or words of doing or being.

Begin every diagram by asking: WHO or WHAT is DOING or BEING something? If you can find only an action, ask: who or what is the doer of it? The SUBJECT is the "doer" or "be-er" of the verb; the VERB is what the subject "does" or "is."

Now draw a horizontal line and divide it with a vertical one. The SUBJECT and all the things that go with it belong on the left side; the PREDICATE (that means the verb and all the things that go with it) goes to the right of the vertical line.

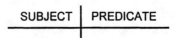

Exercise 2-1: Diagram these sentences.

1. Rex whined.
2. Rex was panting.
3. Rex might have been scratching.
4. Did Rex bark?
5. Should Rex have howled?
6. Rex could have been growling.
7. Rex must have run.
8. Rex had slept.
9. Rex may be eating.
10. Rex will have been digging.

Check your answers. Some new things were thrown at you in this exercise. Did you figure them out? If not, don't worry. We are about to take them up in an orderly manner.

2-A. HELPING VERBS

You have noticed that the verbs in Sentences 2-10 have more than one word. All the words in those sentences except "Rex," which was always the subject, and the very last word, which was the main verb, were HELPING VERBS. Our language shows many fine differences in actions and states of being by the use of helping verbs. For example, "should have been" is a past tense that never happened!

Students who mean business will LEARN the following list of helping verbs:

MAY CAN MUST MIGHT SHALL WILL SHOULD WOULD COULD HAVE DO BE

HAVE includes HAS, HAD, and sometimes HAVING

DO includes DID

BE is a real treasure chest:

AM ARE IS WAS WERE BEING BEEN

Note: HAVE, DO, and BE can be MAIN VERBS, too.

2-B. QUESTIONS

In Sentences 4 and 5, you found that part of the verb came before the subject. Before you diagram a question, you must turn it around to a declarative statement. Change 4 to "Rex did bark." Change 5 to "Rex should have howled." Be careful to include all the helpers in your newly-arranged sentence.

Exercise 2-2: Practice changing questions to declarative statements. (You are not ready to diagram these.)

1. Has Joe been here?
2. Would you have done that?
3. Why did he leave? (This sounds strange turned around: "He did leave why.")
4. Where have you been all day?
5. What can he mean by that statement?
6. Who came to the door?
7. Could Mary be the one we want?
8. Must Alex always be driving his car?
9. Which one did he pick?

10. Whom can a poor girl trust?

Check your answers. If this was very hard, make up some more questions, practice turning them around, and then try the exercise again.

2-C. MODIFIERS: ADJECTIVES AND ADVERBS

Further sentences will be hopelessly boring unless we add some new elements to our study. Let us go back to the definition of a sentence:

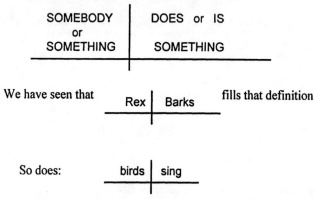

To understand how MODIFIERS work, form a picture in your mind of that sentence, "Birds sing." Are you seeing the birds? Do you imagine them singing? Now hold that picture while we talk about what it means "to modify" something. If you modify a room in your house, you change it, don't you? You rip out a wall or build cupboards. It looks different afterward. That is what our word modifiers do, too. In addition to wanting to know who or what does or is something, we also have questions about the doer and the action or state of being. We want to have our mental picture filled in.

About the BIRDS, we ask:

WHICH ONES?   WHAT KINDS?   WHOSE?   HOW MANY?
These are the ADJECTIVE QUESTIONS.

About the action, SING, we ask:

WHERE?   WHEN?   WHY?   HOW?
These are the ADVERB QUESTIONS.

L*E*A*R*N   T*H*E*M   N*O*W!

You will ABSOLUTELY have to know these questions if you are to learn how to analyze sentences. You will constantly be confronting words and wondering what they are doing in the sentence. You will have to say to yourself, "What question does this answer about what word?" You will not find the right answers unless you learn the **ADJECTIVE AND ADVERB QUESTIONS!**

Now back to your original picture of "Birds sing." How many did you see? If you had seen only two birds and I say "three birds," your picture is <u>modified</u>, or changed, by my ADJECTIVE "three," which told "HOW MANY" birds.

Since ADJECTIVES answer the ADJECTIVE QUESTIONS about NOUNS, they are diagrammed on slanting lines under the noun they modify, thus:

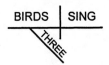

Now notice this sentence.

Those three blue birds sing.

We still have the same subject and verb:

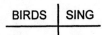

but the subject noun is modified by three words that answer three different ADJECTIVE QUESTIONS.

Exercise 2-3: Diagram the sentence:
Those three blue birds sing.
Tell what question each adjective answers. Then check with the answers in the back of the book.
By the way, the "articles" (as you may have learned to call them) A, AN, and THE, will be considered ADJECTIVES. "A" and "an" tell "how many"; "the" tells "which one."
Can you remember your original picture of "Birds sing"? If I say they were singing "sorrowfully," your picture is modified again. Words ending in "-ly" are usually ADVERBS nearly always answering the ADVERB QUESTION: HOW?

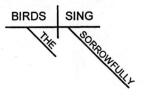

Notice that, while an adjective usually goes in front of its noun, an adverb can hop about in the sentence:

> Sorrowfully the birds sing.
> The birds sorrowfully sing.
> The birds sing sorrowfully.

All three sentences are diagrammed in exactly the same way. (See previous page.)

Exercise 2-4: Diagram these sentences. Put adjectives under nouns, adverbs under verbs. Write what question each modifier answers.

1. Poor Rex whined pitifully.
2. That tired Rex was panting furiously.
3. Yesterday Rex might have been scratching.
4. Did Rex really bark?
5. Why should that naughty Rex have howled so dismally?

There are two tricky things in Sentence 5. First, "why" doesn't <u>answer</u> an adverb question; it <u>is</u> an adverb question. Diagram it just as you would an adverb.

Where did you put "so"? That was really sneaky! It answers the ADVERB QUESTION: HOW. But it does not modify the verb "howled." (How did he howl? So? No.) No, it answers the question "how" about "dismally." (How dismally? <u>So</u> dismally.) Remember that "adverbs modify verbs, adjectives and other adverbs."

So let us take a look at Sentence 5:

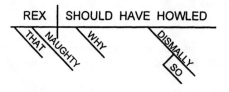

Review and Practice

What have we learned so far?

1. In a sentence, SOMEBODY or SOMETHING DOES or IS SOMETHING.

2.

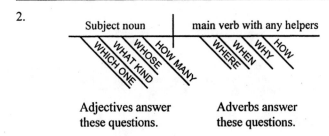

Adjectives answer
these questions.

Adverbs answer
these questions.

3. Before diagramming a question, turn it into a declarative statement, keeping every word.

Exercise 2-5: Diagram these sentences. Be sure to find all helping verbs, and be careful that each modifier is attached to the word it modifies. Don't give up and check the answers till you have tried your best on each item.

1. Harry has been listening carefully.
2. Harry has not been listening carefully.
  (Clue: "not" answers how Harry listens.)
3. Lucy's blue sweater was thrown downstairs.
4. Might that sweet old lady have been sleeping there?
5. Suddenly the booming thunder echoed hollowly.
6. The big bad wolf huffed importantly.
7. What child might be crying now?
8. How they must have been laughing!
9. Away flew the silly geese. (Careful! What IS the verb? What or who DID the verb?)
10. May my sister play here?
11. Who has been whistling?
12. Everyone was sniffling softly.
13. A brilliant sun was streaming everywhere.
14. A very big cookie was being baked.
15. Somewhere fireworks were exploding wildly.
16. Sweetly sings the sparrow.
17. An extremely skinny old cat finally came out.
18. Afterward he talked politely.
19. Now dawn was breaking.
20. Those rather yellow plants have been slowly growing.

After you have checked with the answers, try to figure out why any answer of yours was different. Review the previous material if you had many errors. Chances are mistakes resulted from NOT saying, "What question does this answer?"

2-D. PREPOSITIONS AND PREPOSITIONAL PHRASES

If you want an overview of word groups and their uses in sentences, check the Appendix. If this is all new to you, follow carefully as we explore this territory. If this is review, enjoy it, but make sure you do really know it.

Here are two important definitions:

A **PHRASE** is a GROUP OF WORDS <u>WITHOUT</u> a SUBJECT AND VERB. (It acts as a single part of speech.)
A **CLAUSE** is a GROUP OF WORDS <u>WITH</u> a SUBJECT AND VERB.

All phrases serve as a single part of speech. That means that even though EACH WORD of a prepositional phrase is acting as a certain part of speech, the whole PHRASE may be considered as doing one "job" in the sentence, or being one part of speech.

Prepositional phrases generally serve as either ADJECTIVES or ADVERBS. That means that they will modify NOUNS if they are adjective phrases, or VERBS, ADJECTIVES or other ADVERBS if they are adverb phrases.

What is a preposition? One definition says: "A preposition is anything a squirrel can do to a tree." You will like that if you already know what a preposition is. If you don't, nothing but experience will help. Look up a list of prepositions and learn them if all else fails. Otherwise, carefully consider these examples:

The squirrel ran <u>up</u> the tree, <u>down</u> the tree, <u>behind</u> the tree, <u>through</u> the tree, <u>under</u> the tree, <u>around</u> the tree, <u>into</u> the tree.

All the underlined words connect a noun, "tree," with the rest of the sentence, in this case through the verb "ran." Notice that each prepositional phrase ("phrase" means the preposition, its OBJECT— the noun it connects—and any modifiers of the object) answers the question "where" or possibly "how." These are our old friends, the ADVERB QUESTIONS, and since the phrase answers where and how the verb was carried out, we know these phrases are acting as ADVERBS modifying the verb.

Before we go on to prepositional phrases serving as ADJECTIVES, let's have a look at that squirrel diagrammed:

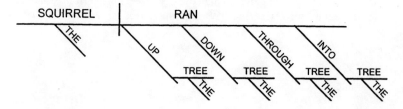

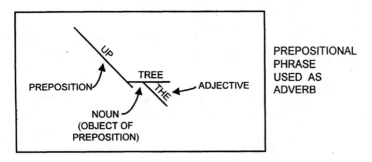

Notice that the preposition goes on a slanting line just below the word the phrase modifies, the object goes on a horizontal line connected to the preposition line, and any modifier of the noun object goes under it. In these phrases the word "the" is an adjective telling "which tree." Even though our word order goes: preposition, adjective, noun object, we diagram it: preposition, noun object, adjective, because we are showing the importance of the words. Tarzan, you see, might say, "Squirrel ran up tree," and we would understand. Newspaper headlines frequently skip words in this manner.

Let us go on to prepositional phrases used as ADJECTIVES.

Exercise 2-6: Think about these sentences. Find the prepositional phrases, decide what question each answers, and diagram the sentences.

1. The boy with the red hat was singing.
2. A basket of food appeared.
3. That cat of Lucy's scratches.
4. An amount of six dollars was owed.

Most prepositional phrases used as adjectives answer the ADJECTIVE QUESTIONS "which one" and "what kind." However, did you notice that in the four sentences above, each adjective question was answered once? If you missed it, go back and look at them again.

Before we review and practice, here is a warning. No, I will go ahead and trick you, and then you will remember better.

Exercise 2-7: Diagram: The bird in the tree sang happily.

You found the prepositional phrase. You asked, "What question does it answer?" and you said "Where," didn't you? What the prepositional phrase "in the tree" really tells is "which one."

It does this by telling "where." Now think about that. We often tell "which one" about a noun in this way. "Which dress will you wear?" "The one on the bed."

NOT the one <u>in the closet</u>, or <u>over the chair</u>, or <u>under the dresser</u>.

This is an example of how you must always THINK about what words and word groups are really doing. In most cases, word order will be a clue as to what a prepositional phrase modifies.

It may be well to notice that, in our speech patterns, while one-word adjectives generally go <u>in front of</u> the nouns they modify, prepositional phrases used as adjectives go <u>after</u> their nouns.

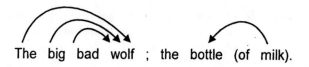

The big bad wolf ; the bottle (of milk).

One final example to study:

The horse with the star on its forehead galloped through the pastures with angry snortings at its pursuers.

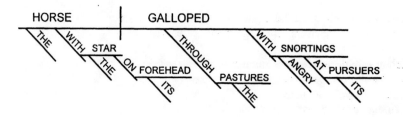

Study the placement of all phrases. Notice "on its forehead" modifies the noun "star." ("On its forehead" does NOT describe this horse!) Nor did it "gallop" "at its pursuers." That tells about its "snortings." Any noun, not just the subject noun, may be modified by a prepositional phrase.

Review and Practice

1. Each word in a sentence is one of the eight parts of speech, depending on the job it does in the sentence.
2. Groups of words, called phrases, may act as single parts of speech.
3. A prepositional phrase consists of a preposition, a noun object, and perhaps some adjectives modifying the object.
4. A preposition connects the object with the rest of the sentence and shows how

the object is related to the sentence. Usually the relationship has to do with direction, space, time, possession, etc.

5. Prepositional phrases usually act as ADJECTIVES or ADVERBS. The whole phrase will answer one of the ADJECTIVE or ADVERB QUESTIONS.
6. We diagram a prepositional phrase under the word it modifies. The object goes on a horizontal line connected to the preposition. Any modifiers of the object go under the object. Example:

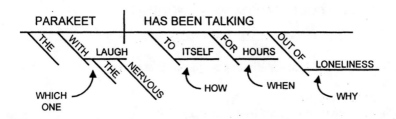

Exercise 2-8: Diagram these sentences after you have found each prepositional phrase and asked yourself, "What question does it answer?"

1. The lamp with the crooked shade leaned against the wall.
2. The carefree moth with the black spots on its wings lunged happily toward the flames of the sooty lantern.
3. The rich society lady sighed with regret over the column in the paper.
4. After the rain Nellie splashed in the puddles on the walk.
5. John had been reading about space travel in that book with the orange cover.
6. Have you ever looked so closely at a bug before tonight?
(Perhaps you should check your answers up to this point and smooth out any problems you may be having.)
7. Suzy has been playing with that girl in the house at the corner.
8. During the winter the farmer worked at repairs in his barn.
9. Should Harry have been sleeping on the porch without a blanket?
10. In January I walk to school in the dark.
11. Beside the dry brook she wept for the thirsty violets.
12. Across the bed lay her beautiful gown.
    (Careful!)
13. Can he really be sleeping through all this noise?
14. His game of tennis was canceled because of rain. (Treat "because of" as one word.)
15. Nobody had been looking toward the mountain with its halo of sunset.
16. What can be known of the outcome?
17. Whose shoe was thrown down the stairs?
18. She laughed about the incident.
19. He sat on a chair with a purple cushion on its seat.

20. With all this practice in diagramming, I am growing in my knowledge of grammar.

2-E. COORDINATING CONJUNCTIONS

There are two kinds of CONJUNCTIONS: **CO**ordinating and **SUB**ordinating.

Coordinating conjunctions join two EQUAL words, phrases, or clauses.

Learn this list of COORDINATING CONJUNCTIONS:

AND BUT OR NOR FOR

Study these examples of coordinating conjunctions at work:

Joe **and** Suzy (two words)
Up the tree **and** down the tree (two phrases)
He went **but** I stayed. (two clauses)
Rain **or** shine—Neither war **nor** peace
(Neither is nearly always used with nor.)

2-F. COMPOUND ELEMENTS

When two or more items are joined by a coordinating conjunction, they form a COMPOUND ELEMENT. Here are some examples of how these things are diagrammed:

Compound subjects:

Compound verbs:

Compound objects of   prepositions:

Compound prepositional
phrases:

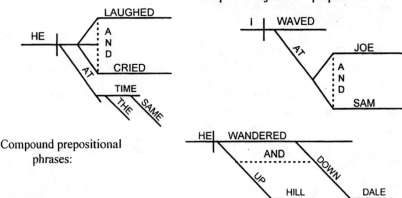

Compound main verbs:

Even compound sentences:

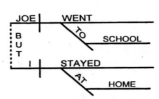

Or combinations:

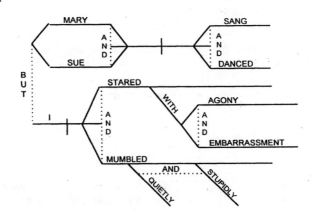

2-G. UNDERSTOOD "YOU"

So far you have always, it is hoped, found the subject of each verb. In every sentence the "doer" or "be-er" of the verb has been stated. However, what about this sentence?

Go!

If a large, fierce person says this to you, you will not stick around looking for a subject. You are immediately aware that the doer of the action is supposed to be "you." That is quickly understood. In fact, we call the subject of a command the "understood 'you'" and we diagram it thus:

$$\underline{\text{(you)} \mid \text{go}}$$

Most commands are given with the subject (you) understood. "Let me alone."

"Give me my purse." "March!" Each of these sentences could have the "you" in front of it, but the receiver of these commands understands without it. Requests, like "Pass the butter, please," also have understood "you" as subject. The "please" is probably an abbreviated condition, "if it pleases you." "Please" is a rather strange word grammatically; you may enjoy considering it further after you finish this book.

2-H. DIRECT ADDRESS

Until now, the only NOUN JOBS you have studied are SUBJECT and OBJECT OF PREPOSITION. There are many more. Now you may add DIRECT ADDRESS. Here are some examples:

> **Mary**, the flowers are blooming.
> Come here, **John**.
> You realize, **Harry**, that I know the truth.

When we call someone by name in a sentence, we are using a NOUN in DIRECT ADDRESS.

This is how such nouns are diagrammed:

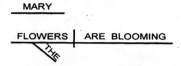

The NOUN of DIRECT ADDRESS has no grammatical connection with the sentence, so it sits on a line above the main clause of the sentence. So does our next item.

2-I. INTERJECTIONS!

An interjection merely expresses emotion; it does no grammatical job in the sentence, so it sits on a line above the sentence, thus:

Wow! Bob fell down the stairs.

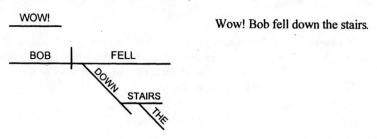

2-J. INTRODUCTORY WORDS

Like nouns of direct address and interjections, certain INTRODUCTORY WORDS have no grammatical connection with the sentence and are diagrammed on a line above the subject.
Examples:

No, he left.   Yes, I stayed.   Well, Rex was barking.

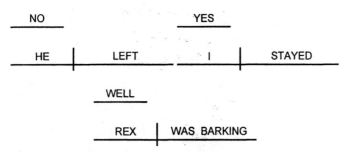

Now you have finished all the basic steps to <u>beginning</u> diagramming. To make sure you have really learned them, the next exercise will review everything covered. Some basics to remember:

1. Make sure you have found all parts of the verb, all the helpers.
2. Pick out prepositional phrases. Determine what question (adjective or adverb) they answer.
3. Check to make sure your diagram makes sense. Is your subject the "doer" or the "be-er" of the verb? Does each modifier answer its question about the word to which you have attached it?

Exercise 2-9: Diagram carefully and check answers in back of book.

1. The wily fox jumped from the stump of the oak tree.
2. Quickly he ran across the sunlit clearing and into the dark forest.
3. Over the river and through the woods to Grandmother's house we go.
4. On the ninth page of the little diary in her bureau drawer was written the secret of the missing fur scarf.
5. Should you have been tapdancing on her new table or singing so loudly?
6. Mitzi and Helen have definitely been studying for Mrs. Smith's dreadful geography test.
7. Very slowly the tired, dirty kitten limped toward home.
8. Must you always be riding on that dangerous motorcycle?
9. Fantastic bargains can be found by early shoppers at the weekend sale of hardware items.
10. Look, Nellie, at the strange, furry creatures under your bed!
11. Alas! I have not dusted there for many weeks.
12. Nellie, you have never dusted under that bed or in your room.

13. Sometimes I wonder at the stupidity of the human race and long for membership in a brighter group.

14. Hah! By such a group you would be eliminated in the first cuts at the tryouts!

15. I am truly amazed by my success at this diagramming business, but I wish for a rest now.

Check your answers and look up any area in which you made a mistake.

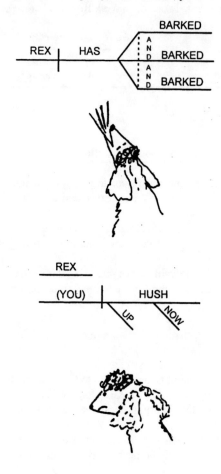

VERBS

TRANSITIVE (Carries action to a receiver)	INTRANSITIVE (Does NOT carry action to a receiver)

TRANSITIVE ACTIVE (TA)

REX | BIT | JOE (TA → DO)

Subject <u>does</u> action.
Direct Object <u>receives</u> action.
(**TA** <u>ALWAYS</u> HAS **DO**)

INTRANSITIVE COMPLETE (IC)

REX | BARKS / at Joe

Action, but <u>no</u> receiver.
Subject <u>does</u> action.

TRANSITIVE PASSIVE (TP)

JOE | WAS BITTEN / by Rex

Subject <u>receives</u> action.

Doer of action, if shown, is in prepositional phrase after "by."

INTRANSITIVE LINKING (IL)

REX | IS \ HAPPY (IL / PA)
REX | IS \ DOG (IL / PN)

<u>No action</u>. Verb acts as equals mark.

Links subject with predicate noun (**PN**) or predicate adjective (**PA**).

MEMORIZE LINKING VERBS:

BE	SOUND
BECOME	TASTE
SEEM	SMELL
APPEAR	REMAIN
LOOK	GROW
FEEL	STAY

ACTION

BEING

CHAPTER THREE
KINDS OF VERBS

Take a look at the chart entitled "VERBS." It shows you that there are four kinds of verbs. They are divided under two headings:

TRANSITIVE and INTRANSITIVE

Remember that you learned that a VERB is a word of ACTION or BEING. Notice that three of the four kinds of verbs are ACTION verbs: Transitive Active, Transitive Passive, and Intransitive Complete. Nearly all the sentences you have diagrammed so far have had Intransitive Complete verbs. The fourth kind is called Intransitive Linking: These are the BEING verbs.

Let us go back to the two main headings: TRANSITIVE and INTRANSITIVE. Memorize these two definitions:

A TRANSITIVE VERB CARRIES ACTION TO A RECEIVER.

AN INTRANSITIVE VERB DOES <u>NOT</u> CARRY ACTION TO A RECEIVER.

You can remember that a transit system is supposed to carry people to a depot or station where they get off the bus or train. A **transitive** verb is in the same business.

The "in-" of "intransitive" means "not," so an intransitive verb simply does NOT carry action to a receiver. (Sometimes that is because there is no <u>receiver</u>; sometimes there is no <u>action</u> to be carried.)

3-A. INTRANSITIVE COMPLETE VERBS

We are starting with the simplest type of verb to understand and to diagram: INTRANSITIVE COMPLETE (IC). Our title, *Rex Barks*, is a sentence with an IC verb. An IC verb has ACTION but NO RECEIVER OF THE ACTION. Rex barks, but he doesn't "bark SOMETHING." Nothing "gets barked." An IC verb can have helping verbs: Rex was barking, has barked, might have been barking, etc. All these are IC verbs. The SUBJECT DOES the action: The ACTION has NO RECEIVER.

Sometimes the action we describe doesn't seem very lively. All these examples are ACTION verbs, all IC:

Rex lay in the kennel. The rat had died in the trap. He existed in a coma. We had been sleeping on the porch.

Also, sometimes there IS a sort of receiver, at least in real life. In the sentence, "Rex barks at Joe," really Joe receives some action from the barking. He must hear it! But not GRAMMATICALLY! "At Joe" is a prepositional phrase telling **how** or **where** or possibly **why** Rex barks. (You knew that already, didn't you?)

As you have been doing, continue to place the verb with all its helpers on the verb line to the right of the subject. But now check to make sure the subject is doing the action and that there is no receiver of the action. Then label such verbs **IC** for INTRANSITIVE COMPLETE.

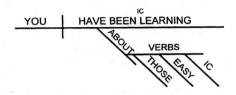

3-B. TRANSITIVE ACTIVE VERBS

If I say to you, "Rex bit," you do not feel I have made a complete sentence, do you? Yet there is a subject (Rex) and a verb (bit). But the thought is not complete. You wait for me to answer the question, "What?" What in the world did Rex bite? Or "Whom?"

So I say, "Rex bit Joe." Now the idea is complete.

Here we definitely have a verb of ACTION. The subject (Rex) DID the action. The action, as poor Joe will quickly agree, has been RECEIVED. We are ready for our first TRANSITIVE ACTIVE (TA) verb:

REX | BIT | JOE

Perhaps you already know the grammatical term for the noun that receives the action of a TRANSITIVE ACTIVE (TA) verb? **DO** stands for DIRECT OBJECT. You will **NEVER** have a TA without a DO; you will **NEVER** have a DO without a TA. The action arrow is not urgently necessary in diagramming, but until you have really mastered verbs, it may be helpful to draw at least a **mental** arrow as you make sure that the SUBJECT really DID THIS VERB to the DIRECT OBJECT. Did Rex DO the biting? Yes. Did Joe RECEIVE the biting? Yes. OK, **TA** and **DO** it is.

Exercise 3-1: Think of a word to fill in each missing element, and label all TA's and DO's. Then diagram the sentences. Remember to put a vertical line just to the base line between the TA verb and the DO.

1. Nellie _____ the dishes in the sink.
2. Have you seen the cat's _____?
3. On Friday all the _____ quit their jobs.
4. I do not believe those _____.
5. Otto _____ food to the squirrels.

You have now studied one kind of INTRANSITIVE verb (IC) and one kind of TRANSITIVE verb (TA). Remember the difference? (Of course you do: IC has no receiver of action; TA has a DO receiver.)

One of the strengths of our language is that it is flexible. We may bend a single word into many uses. And so, you should not be surprised to learn that some verbs can be, in different sentences, EITHER transitive or intransitive.

Here are two sentences. Look at them carefully and see the difference between the verbs.

Rex <u>has been running</u> in the woods.   Rex <u>ran</u> the cat up the tree.

In the first sentence, the verb, "has been running," shows the action Rex did. Did anything RECEIVE the action? No, Rex just did it. "In the woods" is a prepositional phrase telling "where" he did it.

But in the second sentence, Rex ran SOMETHING. Something received the action of his running; something "got run."

Let us diagram these two sentences:

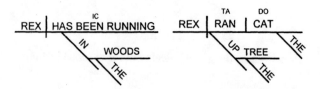

Now you will be ready to understand this explanation:

Have you ever noticed, when you look up a verb in the dictionary, the little letters in italics, v.i. or v.t.? Every verb will have one set of the letters usually placed right after the pronunciation guide. Look up, for example, the verb "run."** It is followed by "v.i." There will be a long definition which may begin: "to move swiftly." Read on through that definition and you should come to "v.t." Then another definition follows, perhaps: "to cause to run."

Let's go back to our two sentences: Rex has been running in the woods. Rex ran the cat up the tree.

Surely you can guess what "v.i." stands for now? "Verb Intransitive," of course. And "v.t." means Verb Transitive.

Check it out. In the first sentence (intransitive) Rex has indeed "been moving swiftly" through the woods. In the second Rex has "caused" the cat "to run." (transitive).

Exercise 3-2: Now examine, diagram, and label these sentences, which give further examples of verbs used both intransitively (NO receiver of the action) and transitively (action has receiver.)

1. Birds sing. Birds sing songs.
2. Bill was fighting. Ali was fighting Joe for the title.
3. Dawn broke over the mountain. Did you break that cup?
4. She swept through the room like a queen. I swept the porch.

Check your answers. Study any errors until you understand what went wrong.

Here is further practice in diagramming sentences containing the two kinds of verbs you have studied: INTRANSITIVE COMPLETE (IC) and TRANSITIVE ACTIVE (TA). Sort them out.

Make sure you don't confuse a modifier with a receiver. A receiver won't be answering ADJECTIVE or ADVERB QUESTIONS, for it will be a NOUN. A DIRECT OBJECT answers "What?" or "Whom?"

Exercise 3-3: Diagram the sentences and label IC, TA and DO where appropriate.

** A verb is referred to in its INFINITIVE form; that is, the one that "to" would introduce: to run, to speak, to be, to crawl, etc. Be aware that this "to" is NOT a PREPOSITION.

1. Rex bit into his toy cat.
2. Rex bit the mailman.
3. Can Rex jump over the fence?
4. Yes, he can jump that fence with no trouble.
5. Where did Rex bury his bone?
6. Eagerly Rex raced toward the barn.
7. That bad Rex has been racing cars again.
8. Should I have tied Rex to the fence?
9. Can you stand his pitiful whining?
10. He escaped yesterday and followed Ann to school.

Now check your answers. If you made mistakes, review this section and make sure you understand what you did wrong.

In the last exercise you were diagramming two of the four kinds of verbs: Intransitive Complete and Transitive Active. There are two more kinds: Transitive Passive and Intransitive Linking. How are you ever going to learn all four kinds? How will you know which verb is which kind? Answer: By T*H*I*N*K*I*N*G!

You will have to follow every step carefully, memorize definitions, and practice thoughtfully.

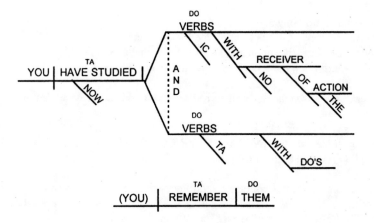

3-C. TRANSITIVE PASSIVE VERBS

Recite the definition of TRANSITIVE VERB. Does it say anything about carrying action FROM A DOER to a receiver? No, indeed. It just says that a TRANSITIVE VERB carries action to a RECEIVER. There is a good reason.

Sometimes the doer of a received action is not known. Sometimes we want to emphasize the receiver of the action. Sometimes we want to hide the doer.

When the dictionary says a verb is "v.t.," it does not know whether the verb will be in the
ACTIVE or PASSIVE VOICE.

The dictionary is only telling you that the verb can be TRANSITIVE, that it can carry action to a RECEIVER.

All the transitive verbs you have studied so far have carried action from a SUBJECT doer of the action to a DIRECT OBJECT receiver of the action:
Rex bit Joe.

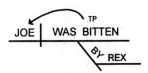

But **hark**! What about this sentence?

Joe was bitten by Rex.

This sentence describes the same action as the first, doesn't it? There is ACTION, some biting going on. There is a DOER of the action, good old Rex. And poor Joe is still RECEIVING the action. What has happened to the sentence? When in doubt, diagram:

JOE | WAS BITTEN
.TP
BY REX

Suddenly, the RECEIVER of the action is the SUBJECT!!! Think about that carefully. Both verbs we studied before always had the SUBJECT DOING the action. Now the SUBJECT is sitting there being acted on.

Consider the sentence: Bob has been hurt!

Is there action? Yes, "to hurt" is an action. Is there a receiver of the action? Yes, Bob received the "hurting." We know, therefore, that "has been hurt" is transitive. Let us diagram the sentence and see whether the verb is ACTIVE or PASSIVE VOICE.

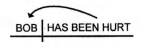

BOB | HAS BEEN HURT

Since Bob, the RECEIVER of the action, is also the SUBJECT of the verb, we know that "has been hurt" is TRANSITIVE PASSIVE (TP). Now, do we know the doer of the action? No, we don't know who or what did the "hurting" to Bob. Yet the sentence is complete. If the doer of the action is shown, it will be the object of the preposition "by" in a prepositional phrase modifying the verb and answering the question "how?"

Bob has been hurt **by the snowball.**

The sentences below have TA verbs. Rewrite each to make it a TP verb. What will become the subject? If you don't figure that out right away, refer to the Verb Chart. See how "Rex bit Joe" (TA-DO) was changed to "Joe was bitten by Rex" (TP). The DO becomes subject of the TP verb.

You will soon see that, while verbs are sometimes without helpers, ALL TP VERBS will have SOME part of the VERB "TO BE." Other helpers may be used, too: Joe was bitten, had been bitten, must have been bitten, etc.

Exercise 3-4: Observe this example:

> **TA   DO   TP**
> Rex <u>chased</u> the cat. The cat <u>was chased</u> by Rex.

You do the same thing; that is, rewrite the sentence in passive voice.

1. Harry lost the ball.
2. The force of the blow had broken the antique safe.
3. Everyone in the room heard the tinkle of breaking glass.
4. All the people had a good time.
5. With the arrival of Harry, we began the rehearsal.

Notice how strange some of them sound when you make them passive. Did you get them all right?

Now try turning TP verbs around to TA. Note: Unless the doer of the action is shown in a "by" prepositional phrase, you will have to make up a doer. Example:

> TP   TA   DO
> The window <u>has been broken</u>!   <u>Somebody</u> broke the window!

Exercise 3-5:

1. Dorothy was hit on the head by the shutter.
2. Often Melinda has been seen at the opera.

3. In some countries girls are guarded by chaperones.
4. George might have been bitten by a spider.
5. Mother, your favorite lamp has been smashed.
   (Remember about wanting to hide the doer?)

Let us see if you are ready to diagram some sentences with active and passive transitive verbs. By the way, you don't worry about active or passive voice in IN-transitive verbs. Diagram each sentence and label each verb TA or TP. Remember: if you have a TA (TRANSITIVE ACTIVE verb) you will ALWAYS ALWAYS ALWAYS have a DO (DIRECT OBJECT). So label the direct objects, too. You don't have to put the arrows for the direction of the action, but be aware that in the ACTIVE voice, the SUBJECT IS <u>ACTIVE</u>; in the PASSIVE voice, the SUBJECT IS <u>PASSIVE.</u> a passive person just sits there and lets life happen to him; the subject of a passive verb just sits there and receives the action.

Exercise 3-6:

1. Harry was writing a letter to Suzy.
2. That letter was written on Thursday.
3. Who stole the pig?
4. This pig was stolen by the piper's son.
5. A good time was had by all.
6. Nelly was overcome with disgust.
7. The criminal might have been caught in another town.
8. Should Mary have been eating so much candy?
9. The battle was won by the courage of the troops.
10. George broke the record for homeruns.

Check your answers. Look closely at any errors. Do you have the wrong word for the subject? Always re-read your diagram "headline" to see if it makes sense. Nearly always it will sound sensible if you have done it correctly. Did you miss a direct object? Ask yourself, "Was the subject 'verbing something'?" In Sentence 1 Harry was writing. Was Harry writing something? Yes, a letter.

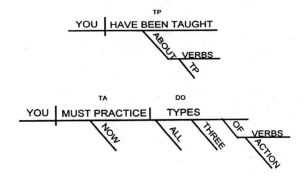

Now that you have studied the three types of action verbs - IC, TA, TP - (and know those symbols so well!) you will have a chance to diagram sentences and determine the types of verbs. First, here are models of the three types:

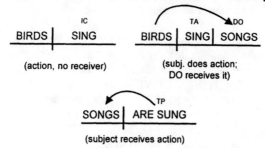

Exercise 3-7: Diagram these sentences carefully. LABEL all verbs and all DIRECT OBJECTS. If action arrows help, draw them.

1. The dog bit the man.
2. The man bit the dog.
3. The dog was bitten by the man.
4. Harry was seen at the opera.
5. Nellie has been riding on her new motorcycle.
6. Cecil came out of the house and jumped into the car.
7. Has Rex been digging up the shrubbery?
   (Careful!)
8. Julia never comes here on Saturday.
9. Nothing could keep Joe away.
10 Have you been visiting Aunt Helen regularly?
11. I have been going there very often.
12. Somewhere I have seen him before.
13. From the kitchen came a clatter of dishes.
14. Why did you tell the secret to Nellie?
15. One perfect rose he gave to me!
16. The paper had been thrown under the porch.
17. Behind the door Brenda was listening carefully.
18. There stood the girl of his dreams.
19. I will neither see him nor be seen with him.
20. With great dignity Rex walked toward the door with the small dog in his mouth.

How well did you do on these? If you were really confused or inaccurate, here are sentences for additional practice. If you feel you are ready to move on, at least look through these sentences to make sure.

Exercise 3-8: All TA and DO but one; find it as you diagram these sentences.

1. He might have found the missing button in the washer.
2. That large mouse has eaten Harry's cheese.
3. Can you see the flag by the dawn's early light?
4. The tuxedo was thrown carelessly on the bed.
5. Beside the road the ducks were eating the grain.

Exercise 3-9: ALL IC or TP; make sure which is which as you diagram and label. (Subject does verb = IC; Verb acts on subject = TP.)

1. Beside the still waters, the sheep were being pastured.
2. Herman has been singing sourly in the shower.
3. The king's presence was awaited in the room.
4. Another storm might have been expected.
5. Might the bundle have fallen off the truck?
6. Suddenly the forest was glowing in the moonlight.
7. Mighty Mouse came to the rescue in time.
8. Could Joe have been pretending?
9. Will her story be remembered?
10. He has forgotten about it completely.

If you have still made errors in this last exercise, study the area that troubles you. If, for example, you labeled a TP verb IC, review TP verbs. Make sure you understand why the answers differ from your work. Prove your case before you decide the answer is wrong.

Before we go on to the fourth and last type of verbs, INTRANSITIVE LINKING, (they are SOOO hard) let us learn one more thing about transitive verbs:

Some TRANSITIVE ACTIVE verbs have INDIRECT OBJECTS. Of course you remember that ALL TA verbs have DO's. But certain verbs of giving, sending, throwing, making, etc., do a tricky thing sometimes. Look at this sentence:

I made a valentine for Suzy.

No indirect object there. Just a good old TA and DO with a prepositional phrase telling <u>for whom</u> I made the valentine. But our language has another way to say this:

I made Suzy a valentine.
It is diagrammed:

See that the diagrams are nearly alike. An (x) takes the place of a missing preposition. The WORD ORDER has changed. When a prepositional phrase telling "to whom" or "for whom" something is done becomes an INDIRECT OBJECT, the preposition disappears and the noun moves BETWEEN the TA and DO. Read these practice sentences carefully. Rewrite where necessary to make INDIRECT OBJECTS. Then diagram the new sentence and label TA, DO, and IO.

Exercise 3-10:

1. I threw the ball to Harry. I threw Harry the ball (Most beginning diagrammers will find themselves "throwing Harry." The ball receives the DIRECT action. It gets thrown. So **ball** is DO.)
2. Did he write a letter to you? Did he write you a letter?
3. By November I had mailed a present to Vernon.
4. He had saved a seat for Ann in the front row.
5. Lottie gives a pain to Mervin.
6. Throw a rope to me!
7. Have you baked a cake for the class?
8. Zelda did knit a sweater for him.

One more way we can put off those INTRANSITIVE LINKING verbs is to study the RETAINED OBJECT. But this is so complicated, you may find it more fun to go on to the IL's. Anyway, you do remember practicing turning TA's to TP's and vice versa? Thus, you could take "I threw Harry the ball" and turn it right around and say, "The ball was thrown TO Harry by me." That would be quite correct. As usual, you made the DO (ball) the subject and then the TP verb (was thrown) carried the action to the subject. Well, sometimes you will see a sentence like this:

Harry was thrown the ball.
Oh! What to do? Well, when in doubt, diagram:

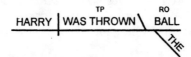

When an INDIRECT OBJECT becomes the SUBJECT of a TP verb, the receiver of the action becomes the RETAINED OBJECT. (This won't happen often.)

Here are some more examples of RETAINED OBJECT so you won't forget it:

Jill was sent money. They had been given many kisses. Joan was handed the problem.

Well, we <u>could</u> learn about objective complements, but no, we'll save them for later and go on to our last and most miserable kind of verb.

3-D. INTRANSITIVE LINKING VERBS

All together now, what were our three kinds of ACTION verbs? Intransitive Complete, Transitive Active and Transitive Passive. Good. But since a VERB is a word of ACTION or <u>BEING</u>, we must have some BEING verbs, and here they are.

If you have studied any grammar, you have probably heard of LINKING verbs. Just remember that their full name is INTRANSITIVE LINKING and label them IL.

Can you guess WHY they are INTRANSITIVE? Because they DO NOT CARRY ACTION TO A RECEIVER.

And why don't they? BECAUSE THERE IS NO ACTION!

We have just covered the easy part.

While many of our sentences in life deal with actions, because we are interested in what things <u>do</u>, we also need a sentence pattern for talking about what a thing IS. We have our five senses, and we wish to express what those senses perceive about things and people. We want to say that

SOMEBODY or SOMETHING	<u>IS</u> SOMETHING

And so we have the INTRANSITIVE LINKING verbs to act as EQUALS MARKS between the SOMEBODY or SOMETHING and the THING or QUALITY it IS.

Study the Verb Chart. At the bottom is a list of INTRANSITIVE LINKING verbs. MEMORIZE THEM NOW. Notice that the first one is BE. Review the many forms that the verb "to be" may take (called **parts** of the verb) and LEARN THEM:

AM ARE IS WAS WERE BEING BEEN

Until now, we have seen the verb "be" and its parts used only as helpers. Now we are ready to use "be" as a main verb. You may have been advised that "be" is not a very strong or interesting verb and now you can see why. It has no ACTION. It doesn't **crash** or **burn** or **dance** or **terrify**. But what would we do without it? Well, perhaps we would sound like Tarzan: "Jane pretty."

With our linking verbs, however, we can express Jane's prettiness with many shades of meaning:
Jane IS (or was or had been, etc.) pretty. Jane BECAME pretty. Jane SMELLS pretty. Jane SEEMED pretty. Jane REMAINS pretty.
Jane APPEARED pretty. Jane GREW pretty (or prettier). Jane STAYED pretty.

We can also have helpers with IL verbs:
Jane <u>MIGHT HAVE BEEN</u> GROWING prettier.

Naturally, if an IL verb is to act as an EQUALS MARK, there has to be something on the other side of the mark. In math you don't leave an equation:
$$2 + 2 =$$
So, just as a TA ALWAYS has a DO (you hadn't forgotten?), an IL verb will be completed by a PREDICATE NOUN (PN) OR PREDICATE ADJECTIVE (PA). The form for the diagram will be:

SUBJECT | IL \ PA   OR   SUBJECT | IL \ PN

Before we forget, since DO's, PA's and PN's COMPLETE the verb, they are called COMPLEMENTS, which means "completers." So two kinds of verbs take COMPLEMENTS. Quick, what are they? TA's and IL's, you say? Right. (Try to keep awake, please.)

Did you notice in the diagram form for IL verbs that the line between IL and PA or PN <u>slants</u>? Unlike the vertical line between TA and DO, which is like a fence, the slanted line before the PA or PN POINTS BACK TO THE SUBJECT. This is very important. Notice:

Are Rex and Joe the same thing?
Or does Joe describe Rex?
Heavens, NO!
(At least not in this sentence.)

Are Rex and dog the same thing?
Yes. <u>Rex equals dog</u> is the message of the sentence.

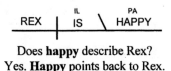

Does **happy** describe Rex?
Yes. **Happy** points back to Rex.

Now that you have MEMORIZED the linking verbs (and repeat them now just to be sure you have), let us take a closer look at how they work.

Not every INTRANSITIVE LINKING verb can take a PN. They can ALL take PA's, however. We showed how **Jane** could EQUAL **pretty**, a PA, with all the IL's that made sense. (She may even have **tasted** pretty, depending on the flavor of her lipstick.) Let's check out which ones can take PN's Make **Jane** EQUAL **cheerleader**. (Don't throw in any "to be's" like "appeared to be a"; infinitives are way down the line.) Fill in the blank with all the IL's that make sense. Remember that you will need to consider the various forms of "be" for the first one.

Exercise 3-11:

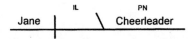

I found four; how many did you get? Check the answers.

Did you notice that the verbs of the five senses wouldn't work? What our senses that perceive how things LOOK, FEEL, SOUND, TASTE and SMELL really do is to answer the ADJECTIVE QUESTION: "What kind?" So they will connect the subject with a PREDICATE ADJECTIVE (PA) only.

Wouldn't it be nice to know that any time you saw one of your dozen IL verbs you could pin it down with an IL label? Alas! You have to make **sure** that it is really being an EQUALS MARK between a subject and a PA or PN.

When one of the verbs on the IL list is used as another type of verb (IC, TA, or TP), the MEANING of the verb has changed somewhat. Observe:

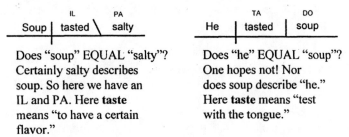

Does "soup" EQUAL "salty"?
Certainly salty describes
soup. So here we have an
IL and PA. Here **taste**
means "to have a certain
flavor."

Does "he" EQUAL "soup"?
One hopes not! Nor
does soup describe "he."
Here **taste** means "test
with the tongue."

Exercise 3-12: First let's diagram some sentences where **all** the verbs are IL. You will have to decide whether the COMPLEMENT is PA or PN. Label verbs and complements and make sure the line between slants toward the subject.

1. She has been looking sick lately.
2. I am becoming angrier by the minute.
3. The trees in the Blue Ridge Mountains do look blue.
4. After the game, Nancy and Helen sounded very unhappy.
5. This corn must have been fresher yesterday.
6. Can the lake have appeared this blue before?
7. That old man has remained our club's president for years.
8. In Nellie's eyes, Harry is a prince.
9. The actor seemed young at first but grew older during the play.
10. Should he always be the winner of every race?

Exercise 3-13: After you have checked your answers, make sure you understand any errors you made. Now we will look at some sentences that show verbs from our IL list doing other things. This will be a good review of IC, TA, and TP verbs. Diagram and label all verbs and complements. See how the verb is used differently from the way it was used as IL.

1. The beggar looked in the window.
2. Suddenly he appeared at the door.
3. Rex smelled the stranger.
4. The fireman sounded the alarm.
5. The pudding had been tasted by the cook.
6. Herman grew rapidly. Herman grew carrots.
7. Stay away from me!
8. That dress really becomes you.
9. The three blind men carefully felt the elephant.
10. Is the doctor in his office?

That last one is peculiar, isn't it? Diagrammed, it seems to be an IC. But if you read the "headline," (doctor is), you feel something is not complete. The sentence really needs the adverbial prepositional phrase, "in his office," to complete the meaning. But that phrase answers "where?" Well, who ever said the English language wasn't full of variety?

Exercise 3-14: Now you will have to sort out a mixture. Diagram these sentences. Label verbs and complements, test your "headlines" to see if they make sense, and use mental action arrows and equals marks to make sure you did them properly.

1. Rex grew more nervous in the crowd.
2. Cotton has been grown on this land for years.

3. Before the flood, the city had been growing normally.
4. The murderer might have grown a beard since the crime.
5. Popeye smelled spinach and felt hopeful.
6. Edna remained a housewife throughout her marriage.
7. The king became angry but stayed his hand.
8. His wrath had been felt by the people.
9. She might be becoming slim <u>because of</u> her diet.
10. He had been a frog but became a prince.

How did you do on those? What did your errors show you? If you are feeling desperate, review the Verb Chart. Then reread the introductory material for each type of verb and try a few of the exercises. Perhaps studying the answer section will give you the most help. Look up WHY each thing is where it is.

And if you did well in all this, HOORAY!

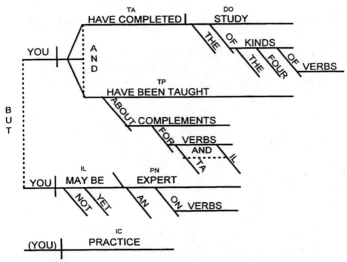

Review and Practice: Diagram, label, and check answers.

Exercise 3-15: IC Verbs (Action but no receiver.)

1. Those naughty twins have been jumping on the sofa again.
2. Out the window flew the parakeet.
3. Does that young man still believe in the Easter Bunny?
4. Where can he be going at this hour?
5. Clara should not have been wading in the brook.

Exercise 3-16: TA Verbs (Action carried to DO receiver.)

1. Must we carry those heavy baskets to town?
2. That slender girl has thrown the discus for a record distance.
3. She might have sent me the money in the letter. (IO!)
4. Quietly she smelled the sweet aroma of the gardenia.
5. In the last race he had seriously hurt his chances of winning.

Exercise 3-17: TP Verbs (Subject receives action.)

1. A message in a crumpled paper was dropped at her feet.
2. Can such an outrage be allowed?
3. Bill's speech was received by the student body with cheers.
4. The letter had been opened earlier by another Mr. Smith.
5. The ad should not have been published until Friday.

Exercise 3-18: IL Verbs (Equals mark between subject and PN or PA.)

1. The rain felt cool and the breeze smelled fresh.
2. Through all the trouble, Norman has remained my friend.
3. That official has always been surly and arrogant toward us.
4. Might she have become queen of her native country?
5. Look neat, be polite, appear cheerful, and stay healthy.

Exercise 3-19: Mixed Verbs.

1. I can eat anything except liver.
2. Could you possibly be silent for one minute?
3. What did he see at the circus?
4. He was ushered to a front seat.
5. Since yesterday Harry has been constantly thinking about her.
6. At the very end of the highest branch of the apple tree perched the cat.
7. Paul's sweater was lost at the station, but no one turned it in.
8. The careless driver was speeding past the police car.
9. Loosen your tie, take your shoes off, and relax.
10. I feel bad about your loss of your favorite easy chair.

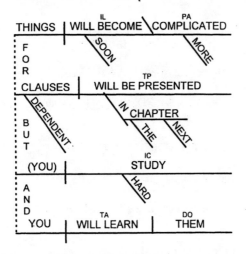

CHAPTER FOUR
DEPENDENT CLAUSES

What is a CLAUSE? Memorize these two definitions:

A **PHRASE** is a GROUP OF WORDS <u>WITHOUT</u> a subject and verb, used as a SINGLE PART OF SPEECH.

A **CLAUSE** is a GROUP OF WORDS <u>WITH</u> a SUBJECT and VERB.

You have already studied TWO kinds of PHRASES:

1. VERB PHRASE - a main verb and all its helpers. (Example: Rex <u>has been chasing</u> cars.)

2. PREPOSITIONAL PHRASE - a preposition, its object, and any modifiers of the object. (Example: Rex ran <u>through the dark woods.)</u>

Notice that a verb <u>phrase</u> has no subject within it. But a SENTENCE always has a subject and a verb. SO every sentence you have studied so far has BEEN a CLAUSE.

That means you have already been studying ONE kind of clause:

1. MAIN or INDEPENDENT CLAUSE—a group of words WITH a SUBJECT and VERB that can STAND ALONE.

Now you will study:

2. DEPENDENT or SUBORDINATE CLAUSE—a group of words WITH SUBJECT and VERB that CAN **NOT** STAND ALONE and that is used as a SINGLE PART OF SPEECH.

For an overview of PHRASES and CLAUSES, you may wish to look at the Appendix. It is a good idea to keep reviewing the total picture. But now we must dig into the specifics.

May we assume that you understand that a SENTENCE ALWAYS includes AT LEAST ONE MAIN CLAUSE? For a SENTENCE is "a group of words WITH SUBJECT and VERB expressing a COMPLETE thought."

But now we must learn about GROUPS OF WORDS with SUBJECT and VERB that **CANNOT** STAND ALONE.

Why does our language need such a construction? Let us think back to our study of MODIFIERS. We found we needed MORE INFORMATION about our subjects and verbs. First we studied one-word modifiers:

Rex barked <u>yesterday.</u>

"Yesterday" is a one-word ADVERB answering "When?"

But suppose we wanted to be more specific:

Rex barked <u>in the afternoon.</u>

For this information we needed a prepositional phrase. It includes a preposition, a noun object, and an adjective modifying the object. The whole PHRASE is used as a SINGLE PART OF SPEECH, namely an ADVERB answering "When?"

Now look carefully at this:

Rex barked <u>when the mailman came.</u>

We now have something with a conjunction, adjective, noun, and verb. But it is a unit. Did the "mailman" do the "coming"? Yes, so we have a SUBJECT and VERB.

What we have in "when the mailman came" is A GROUP OF WORDS
1) with SUBJECT AND VERB
2) that CANNOT STAND ALONE (try it) AND
3) that IS USED AS A SINGLE PART OF SPEECH (an adverb that answers "When?")

That is exactly the definition of a DEPENDENT or SUBORDINATE CLAUSE!

Let's review:

When did Rex bark?   Yesterday. (An adverb.)
When did Rex bark?   In the afternoon. (An adverb phrase.)
When did Rex bark?   When the mailman came. (An adverb clause.)

Were you bothered to see a PREPOSITIONAL PHRASE called an ADVERB PHRASE, or a DEPENDENT CLAUSE called an ADVERB CLAUSE? That is just like saying, "I am from the USA" and "I am from Virginia." One is a unit contained within another, thus:

PREPOSITIONAL PHRASES
    Adverb phrases
    Adjective phrases

DEPENDENT or SUBORDINATE CLAUSES
    Adverb clauses
    Adjective clauses
    Noun clauses

By the way, let's not worry about DEPENDENT and SUBORDINATE. They mean the same thing and the terms are interchangeable.

MAIN and INDEPENDENT are also interchangeable.

We will begin with the easiest kind of dependent clause.

4-A. ADVERB CLAUSES

We have just studied an example of an adverb clause:

Rex barked when the mailman came.

Here is how we diagram it:

Read through these sentences and find the adverb clauses:

1. Rex barked after the mailman left.
2. Rex barked because he hates the mailman.
3. Rex barked until the sun went down.
4. If he does not stop barking, Rex will be very sorry.
5. Since Rex started barking, three people have called.

If you were playing detective, what could you learn about adverb clauses from those five sentences? Go back and study them some more. You may wish to diagram them. Then compare your list of findings with mine.

1. Adverb clauses answer "why?" and some other strange things. What question does "if" answer? It tells something like "under what circumstances?" (We can lump such adverb clauses under things that tell "how.")

2. Adverb clauses are introduced by a connecting word. These sentences had after, because, until, if, and since.

3. Adverb clauses, like other adverbs, may move to the front of the sentence. In Sentences 4 and 5 the adverb clauses came first.

4. When the adverb clause comes first, it is followed by a comma.

That is what you could have observed from the five examples. Did you find it all? Did you find anything else? You might have noticed that "after" is sometimes a preposition. Compare these two:

Rex ran after the ball.   Rex barked after the mailman came.

The first "after" is a PREPOSITION.   The second "after" is a:
SUBORDINATING CONJUNCTION
introducing an ADVERB CLAUSE.

There are many, many subordinating conjunctions. You can make your own list by seeing how many words make sense on the conjunction line, a dotted line joining the word the clause modifies and the adverb clause itself.

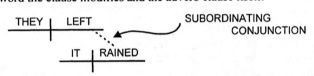

The word "subordinating" means "making something of lower rank." See what SUBORDINATING CONJUNCTIONS do to these sentences:

1. The mailman came. When the mailman came
2. He left. After he left
3. Nellie caught the ball. Because Nellie caught the ball
4. You don't pay attention. If you don't pay attention

The first group in each case CAN stand alone. We may desire more information about the sentence "He left." But we will be satisfied to wait for another sentence to find out when, why, etc.

But suppose someone comes into the room and says any of those second parts. You want to know, "Well, what?" What happened when the mailman came? What happened after he left? The addition of just one word, the SUBORDINATING

CONJUNCTION, made us aware that the idea in the clause was not complete, that the MAIN information was missing.

So we have seen that a subordinating conjunction **subordinates**. We also know that a conjunction **joins**. Remember the definition: A CONJUNCTION joins two words, phrases, or CLAUSES.

Do you remember learning this? (way back)

There are two kinds of CONJUNCTIONS:

> COORDINATING—joins two EQUAL words, phrases or clauses
> (AND, BUT, OR, NOR, FOR)
> SUBORDINATING

You can now fill in a definition for SUBORDINATING. How about "introduces an adverb clause and joins it to a main clause."

Exercise 4-1: Diagram these and check your answers. Notice that every sentence has a MAIN clause. Make sure the main clause is on top in your diagram.

1. While Nero fiddled, Rome burned.
2. She laughed after he turned his back.
3. If winter comes, can spring be far behind?
4. Rex hides in the closet whenever it thunders.
5. When money talks, I listen.
6. As you stand up, the group will sit down.
7. I danced until the musicians were tired.
8. Whither thou goest, I will go.
9. Although I don't like him, I must be kind to him.
10. I came because you called.

These are certainly easy, aren't they? But you knew something would complicate things, didn't you? There are several tricky things which can be put under the heading of

ELLIPTICAL CLAUSES

An elliptical expression is one which has some words left out. (Now don't ask me why it is called that.)
Notice these sentences:
> Nellie is taller than Harry.

Nellie is as tall as Mary.
Here is how they are diagrammed:

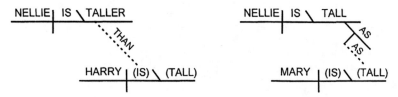

You might have thought that "than Harry" was a prepositional phrase. Not so! "Than" is ALWAYS a conjunction. It nearly always introduces an elliptical clause. If you understand that, you can figure out the difference between these two sentences.

You like Millie better than I.   You like Millie better than me.

Diagramming is the best way to illustrate the difference:

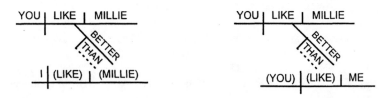

While you can count on "than" to be a conjunction, "as" is much trickier. It often comes in pairs, as it did in the example:

Nellie is as tall as Mary.

Here is how your thoughts should run as you diagram that. "Nellie" is the subject of "is." "Tall" seems to be an adjective that completes "is." So

NELLIE| IS \ TALL

is the main clause. Now, **how** "tall"? "As" tall. Hmmm.

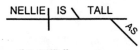

How "as"? As tall "as Mary (is) (tall)."

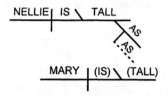

The FIRST "as" is an ADVERB modifying "tall" all by itself. This "as" is a special kind of adverb that needs a modifying clause introduced by another "as," this time a subordinating conjunction. Isn't that awful?

Exercise 4-2: Let's diagram some elliptical clauses for practice.

1. Harry can sing louder than Mike can.
2. Can Suzy play the piano as well as Joe?
3. We stayed there longer than here.
4. He came as quickly as he could.
5. Mother gave you more money than me. (Remember IO?)

Did you observe that "than" and "as" clauses could modify something other than action verbs? Remember that ADVERBS can modify VERBS, ADJECTIVES, and other ADVERBS. Go back and see what "than" and "as" clauses modified: ADJECTIVES like "tall" and "taller," ADVERBS like "louder" or even "as."

Exercise 4-3: We need one more practice on adverb clauses. Diagram these and check your answers.

1. Before Bill arrived, we hid behind the sofa.
2. We jumped out when he came and surprised him.
3. After the party was over, we cleaned the house, since it was a mess.
4. We overslept because the time had changed in the night.
5. I do a better thing than I have ever done.
6. He went where seldom is heard a discouraging word.
7. As the twig is bent, the tree is inclined.
8. He gave me food when I was hungry.
9. Though He slay me, yet will I trust Him.
10. If you see Mabel, say "Hi."

Do you have these pretty well conquered? Notice that you have to remember all the other things you learned. That last practice included all types of verbs, some compound elements, an understood "you," as well as the new material.

Do not proceed to the next area until you really feel you know adverb clauses. Study the answers. Reread the explanations. Try the exercises again.

4-B. ADJECTIVE CLAUSES

Dependent clauses can be:
> —ADVERB CLAUSES
> —ADJECTIVE CLAUSES
> —NOUN CLAUSES

An ADJECTIVE CLAUSE is a

> —DEPENDENT CLAUSE (group of words with subject and verb which can't stand alone and which is used as a single part of speech)
> —USED AS AN ADJECTIVE (word which modifies a noun or pronoun, telling "WHICH ONE, WHAT KIND, WHOSE, HOW MANY")

Perhaps you didn't need all that review? Let us proceed.

An ADJECTIVE CLAUSE is introduced by a RELATIVE PRONOUN:
WHO WHOSE WHOM THAT WHICH

Look at this sentence:
> The dog that barked is Rex.

Here is how it is diagrammed:

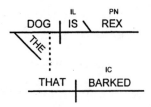

Suppose you play detective again. How did that sentence differ from a sentence with an adverb clause?

1. There is a dotted line, but it is vertical and nothing is written on it.
2. A relative pronoun hangs on the end of the dotted line.
3. If you substitute the word above the dotted line for the word at the bottom of the dotted line, it makes sense: "dog barked."
4. While an <u>adverb</u> clause seemed to come at the beginning of the sentence or

after the main clause, this <u>adjective</u> clause came between the subject and the verb of the main clause. It came RIGHT AFTER THE NOUN IT MODIFIED.

If you didn't discover all those things, learn them now. Nearly all of them apply to every sentence with an adjective clause in it.

Follow these directions as you diagram sentences with adjective clauses:

1. Find the main clause. Diagram it.
2. HANG THE RELATIVE PRONOUN from the noun or pronoun it refers to.

3. Find the adjective clause. Diagram it with reference to the relative pronoun.
4. Substitute the noun or pronoun at the top of the dotted line for the relative pronoun. Does it make sense?

Exercise 4-4: Diagram according to directions.

1. The dog that followed me was wagging its tail.
2. People who live in glass houses should not throw stones.
3. He who hesitates is lost.
4. I met the lady who called us.
5. She called about the car that had been sold.

Check your answers and notice why you made mistakes. Did you follow the directions exactly? Did you HANG the relative pronoun from the thing it referred to? Or when you got to Sentence 4, did you think the "who" had to hang from the subject? An adjective clause can modify ANY noun or pronoun in the sentence, even, as in Sentence 5, a noun that is the object of a preposition.

Notice once more the direction (3) that says: Find the adjective clause. Diagram it WITH REFERENCE TO THE RELATIVE PRONOUN.

What can that mean? Here is a sentence to illustrate:

I have found the cap that I lost.

Main Clause: I have found the cap.

Diagram:

Hang the relative pronoun:

Now, diagram the adjective clause with reference to the relative pronoun. Let's see. The adjective clause is "that I lost." The verb is "lost." But if I put "lost" after "that," and substitute "cap" for "that," I have the "cap" doing the losing. No, something's wrong. What IS the subject of "lost"? Who did the losing in "that I lost"? Why, "I" did! OK, but what happens to "that"? Hmm. If I substitute "cap" for "that," I could say "I lost CAP." That makes sense. So why not diagram it:

And that is what Rule 3 means. Figure out the job the RELATIVE PRONOUN is doing IN ITS OWN CLAUSE! In this case it was being the DIRECT OBJECT. Yet look at what happened to the word order. Here are a number of adjective clauses with the same construction:

that I found, whom he saw, which he took, that we wanted

All of these would be diagrammed the same way. HANG the relative pronoun, then figure out what it's doing in the adjective clause. Let's see if you really can apply the rule.

Exercise 4-5: Diagram:

I have lost the friend in whom I trusted.

Did you get this far?
Then ask what is "whom" doing
in its own clause
Check the answers to see if you got it right.

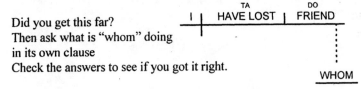

Let's have a look at those relative pronouns again. WHO, WHOSE, and WHOM are three CASES of the same word.

WHO is NOMINATIVE CASE (used for subjects and predicate nominatives)
WHOSE is POSSESSIVE CASE (showing ownership)
WHOM is OBJECTIVE CASE (used for objects of verbs or prepositions.)

WHOSE never gives you a problem in English, unless you confuse it with "who's," a contraction of "who is." But remember where you met WHOSE before? It is an ADJECTIVE QUESTION! So when WHOSE is a relative pronoun, hang it on a SLANTED line and put the noun it modifies above it, thus:

The boy whose bike was stolen cried.

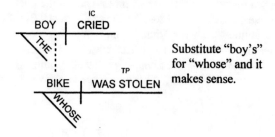

Substitute "boy's" for "whose" and it makes sense.

While WHOSE is easily taken care of, WHO and WHOM are a constant source of irritation. Now that you understand subjects and objects and predicate nominatives, you can always figure out the correct case. When WHO and WHOM are used in main clauses, just see what jobs they are doing. (They are just pronouns, not <u>relative</u> pronouns in main clauses.)

> Who goes there? (Subject, so nominative)
> Whom did you see? (You did see whom. DO, so objective)
> Whom did he ask about? (He did ask about whom. Obj. of prep., so objective.)
> This is who? (Predicate nominative, so nominative)

When WHO or WHOM is a relative pronoun, its CASE depends on its use in ITS <u>OWN</u> CLAUSE.

I know the man who yelled.

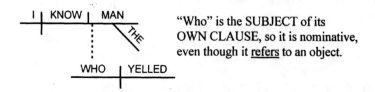

"Who" is the SUBJECT of its OWN CLAUSE, so it is nominative, even though it <u>refers</u> to an object.

A man whom I knew yelled.

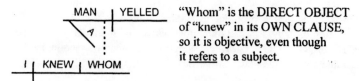

"Whom" is the DIRECT OBJECT of "knew" in its OWN CLAUSE, so it is objective, even though it <u>refers</u> to a subject.

Now you can amaze your friends with your certainty about WHO and WHOM.

The WHO family (WHO, WHOSE, and WHOM) refer to people.
WHICH refers to things.
THAT refers to people OR things.

So much for relative pronouns. Let's practice some sentences with adjective clauses.

Exercise 4-6:

1. The lawn that he had mowed still looked ragged.
2. Did you see the package that arrived?
3. I received the answer for which I had waited.
4. This house is the one that was vandalized.
5. The kitten which was lost was found behind the door which had been shut.
6. The lady whose number was called screamed with delight.
7. The girls, who had been waiting patiently for hours, giggled and shouted when the singer came.
8. The person whom you gave the ring to lost it.
9. Henry knows the villain who shaved off his beard while he was asleep.
10. This is the cat that killed the rat that ate the malt that lay in the house that Jack built.

Check your answers carefully. If you had trouble, review the steps in diagramming these adjective clauses.

There is one more miserable complication to bring in before we finish with ADJECTIVE CLAUSES. Guess what? SOMETIMES THE RELATIVE PRONOUN ISN'T THERE!!
Observe:
The book that I want is missing.
The book I want is missing.

Both sentences are equally correct. Both are clear in meaning. Both are diagrammed in exactly the same way, EXCEPT that you have to supply the missing RELATIVE PRONOUN. You have to HANG a pronoun that isn't there!

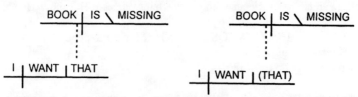

These little pronoun-less adjective clauses go by so quickly that it is hard to catch them. But once you notice that there is an extra subject and verb at large in a sentence, you can ask yourself if it is answering the ADJECTIVE QUESTION "Which one?" and if it is, see if a relative pronoun will fit into the sentence. Here are some sentences with MISSING RELATIVE PRONOUNS.

Exercise 4-7: Diagram:

1. The bird I saw is the bird you described.
2. I heard about the money you saved.
3. I remember the songs he sang, the words he spoke, the promises he made.

4. The house you were born in has been torn down.
5. The life you save may be your own.

If you were able to do these correctly, you will be able to diagram ADJECTIVE CLAUSES <u>with</u> the relative pronouns, too. But probably we had better practice some more, so. . .

Exercise 4-8: Diagram these sentences. Remember the procedure for finding the main clause and HANGING THE RELATIVE PRONOUN from the word it replaces.

1. The one I love belongs to somebody else.
2. Do you know anybody with the nerve he has?
3. After the rain, we resumed the game that we had started.
4. We gasped at the price that had been paid.
5. Nellie's antique cabinet, which had been sold for $500, was appraised at $5000.
6. Mrs. Jones, who was chairman of the committee, asked for silence.
7. The messenger whom you expected never arrived.
8. John, whom they awaited, never came.
9. They elected my sister, whose name had not been among the nominees.
10. They chose a person who had never held office.

How did you do this time? These are really hard; if you did well, you should be pleased, but don't be discouraged if you have to begin again at GO. Study the answers to see how the sentences are really put together.

In the last exercises, did you notice anything about commas? In some sentences the adjective clauses are surrounded by commas; in others they are not. Why?

Did you ever hear of
RESTRICTIVE or NON-RESTRICTIVE CLAUSES?

They are sometimes called
ESSENTIAL or NON-ESSENTIAL CLAUSES.

You will hear about them now.

First you need to know what an ANTECEDENT is. An ANTECEDENT is the word to which a pronoun refers. If I say
Harry rode his bike

the ANTECEDENT of the pronoun "his" is "Harry." The word a RELATIVE PRONOUN HANGS from is its ANTECEDENT. Got it?

Now, listen carefully. When the ADJECTIVE CLAUSE is NECESSARY to identify the ANTECEDENT of the RELATIVE PRONOUN, the ADJECTIVE CLAUSE is called RESTRICTIVE or ESSENTIAL. It is NOT set off by commas.

But, when the ANTECEDENT of the RELATIVE PRONOUN is clearly identified WITHOUT the adjective clause, and when the adjective clause merely gives extra information about the ANTECEDENT, the ADJECTIVE CLAUSE is called NON-RESTRICTIVE or NON-ESSENTIAL, and it is set off by commas.

That takes a while to grasp. But think of the oyster who finds a grain of sand in his shell. He doesn't need it so he builds something around it to set it off. COMMAS around a NON-RESTRICTIVE CLAUSE are like the oyster's PEARL around the UNNECESSARY GRAIN OF SAND. (That is one of my favorites.)

To make sure you understand this, look at the last exercise. The first sentence with a non-restrictive clause is Number 5. Nellie had only one antique cabinet. She did not have several, causing us to identify a certain one by the price at which it sold. No, we knew the exact cabinet. The adjective clause gives us interesting information, important information in understanding the whole sentence. But we do not need it to identify the ANTECEDENT of WHICH, "cabinet."

Normally, antecedents that are proper names will have non-restrictive clauses. Notice Sentences 7 and 8. In 7 we need to know **which** messenger. But in 8 we all know John. Sentences 9 and 10 illustrate the same contrast. "My sister" is known; "person" is not.

Perhaps you had better confront some sentences which have **both** ADJECTIVE and ADVERB CLAUSES. Make sure you have them sorted out before we come to NOUN clauses, which are just dreadful.

Exercise 4-9: Diagram carefully.

1. On the floor lay the drops of wax that had run down from the candle.
2. Wherever he traveled, he met people whom he knew.
3. Because we lost the address he had sent, we did not go.
4. When the helicopter comes, the help for which they have been praying will arrive.
5. That salad is bigger than the one I brought.
6. While you were asleep, the tooth fairy took the tooth you lost.
7. No one who has never been sick can understand the pain he feels.
8. If you like, we can play the records you brought.
9. Benedict Arnold, whose name stands for treason, has not been forgotten by history.
10. The design which won was ugly, although it was expensive.

They are like puzzles, aren't they? By now you know whether you like these puzzles or not. But even if you don't fully enjoy this challenge, which is rather like math, surely you are beginning to appreciate the complexity of your own speech. And there's much more to come!

4-C. NOUN CLAUSES

Here we are buried deep in a study of DEPENDENT CLAUSES. Remember the three varieties:

> —ADJECTIVE
> —ADVERB
> —NOUN

Unlike adjective and adverb clauses, which are **modifiers**, NOUN clauses will be free to do many things in the sentence. They will be doing NOUN jobs.

So far, you have studied several NOUN jobs. Nouns can be

> —SUBJECTS
> —DIRECT OBJECTS
> —INDIRECT OBJECTS
> —OBJECTS OF PREPOSITIONS
> —PREDICATE NOMINATIVES

and some other things.

Well, a NOUN CLAUSE is a DEPENDENT CLAUSE that can do a NOUN job.

Let us start with an example:

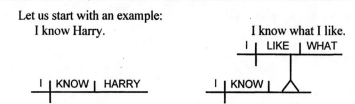

In the first sentence "Harry," a noun, is the direct object of the verb "know." "Harry" receives the action of the "knowing"; he is what "gets known."

In the second sentence, what "gets known"? The WHOLE CLAUSE, "what I like." Since the CLAUSE is the direct object, and since a direct object is a noun job, "what I like" is a NOUN CLAUSE. Ah, if it were all that simple. . .

Notice that there is a pronoun, "what," that seems to introduce the noun clause in the same way a relative pronoun introduced an adjective clause. But "what" is not a relative pronoun, for it does not refer to any noun in the sentence. It stands for the things the speaker likes. Suppose it stands for, let's see, "hamburgers." Suppose we had the sentence:

I know I like hamburgers.

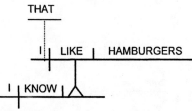

Then look at this:

I know THAT I like hamburgers.

```
THAT
    ┊
   I │ LIKE │ HAMBURGERS
     │
I │ KNOW │ ╱╲
```

Well, where would YOU put an extra "that"?

Let's pull this together. What we have just seen is that

1) Sometimes direct object noun clauses begin with a pronoun that does a job in its own clause (like "what")

2) Sometimes the DO noun clause has NO introductory pronoun ("I like hamburgers")

3) Sometimes DO noun clauses have an extra "that" which just sits on a "skyhook."

Before we get into noun clauses doing other noun jobs, let's diagram some noun clauses used just as direct objects.

Exercise 4-10:

1. I heard what you said. I saw what you did.
2. Did Nancy remember that you had called?
3. They should eat whatever you have cooked.
4. I know whom I have believed.
5. Could Mary be wishing she had not come?
6. He said, "I like Sally."
7. "I like Sally," he said.
8. "I," he replied, "like Sally."
9. Take what you can get your hands on.
10. Do you finally understand what I am talking about?

Those were not too hard, were they? Notice in 6, 7, and 8 that a direct quotation is the direct object of the attributive phrase (the "he said") no matter what the word order.

Before going on to noun clauses that AREN'T direct objects, perhaps we should look at some DO noun clauses that look adverbial.

I saw how he ate. I remember where he lives. I can guess why he left. I noticed when he arrived.

The verbs "saw," "remember," "guess," and "noticed" are all TA verbs. The noun clauses which follow them are all DO's telling WHAT got seen, remembered, etc. Here is one diagrammed:

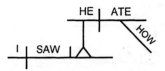

Now you must use your brain and figure out what different NOUN JOBS are done by the following NOUN CLAUSES. Figure out how they should be diagrammed and then check with the answers.

Exercise 4-11:

1. Candy is what he likes.
2. What he likes is candy.

3. I care about what he likes.
4. You gave what he likes no consideration. (A nasty one.)

If you recalled the other noun jobs mentioned earlier in this section, you should have found a noun clause for each job. If you are completely lost, we'll go through it step by step.

Candy is Joe's favorite food.
Candy is what Joe likes best.

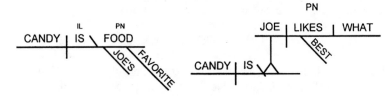

In the first sentence, a plain old noun is the PREDICATE NOMINATIVE. But in the second, the whole noun clause is the PREDICATE NOMINATIVE.

Remember that an IL verb is an EQUALS MARK? You know we can say either 2+2=4 or 4=2+2. So rewrite the second sentence to read:

What Joe likes best is candy.

Now you have a noun clause being SUBJECT of the sentence.

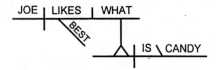

Here are two more sentences:

Pay attention to Greg.
Pay attention to what he says.

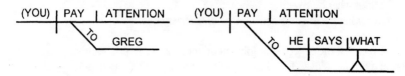

Both sentences have an object for the preposition "to." The first is the noun, "Greg." The second is the noun clause, "what he says." Like the other noun clauses, this one has its own elevated platform.

If you got the fourth sentence right, you have probably taken the rest of the day off to celebrate. That was an awkward and unusual construction:

> You gave what he likes no consideration.

What if it had said: You gave Nellie no consideration. Would you have recognized "Nellie" as an indirect object? By now you have seen this sentence diagrammed thus:

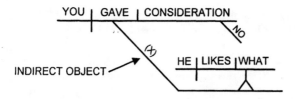

You have been shown NOUN CLAUSES used as SUBJECTS, PREDICATE NOMINATIVES, DIRECT OBJECTS, OBJECTS OF PREPOSITIONS, and INDIRECT OBJECTS. You have seen them introduced by "what," which performs a job in the noun clause itself, by "that," which merely says, "A clause is coming," and by nothing at all.

Exercise 4-12: Diagram the following sentences and check your answers. Tell what noun job each noun clause is doing.

1. What you see is what you get.
2. The truth is that I am penniless.
3. The whole town is gossiping about what Nellie did.
4. We gave no thought to where he went.
5. We gave where he went no thought.
6. That I worried about you is no secret.
7. Jerry shouted that the roof was caving in.
8. Tentatively she decided what was best.
9. That Nellie lied about what she knew was what we learned.
10. That box might have been what he ordered.

Now it is time to put it all together: NOUN, ADJECTIVE, and ADVERB CLAUSES. These sentences will require you to use everything you have learned so far!

Exercise 4-13:

1. While Rex was barking, the thief was stealing the box on the porch.
2. The only thing that was in the box was trash we had collected in the attic.
3. Why no one listened to Rex, I'll never know!
4. The box that had been stolen was later found down the street.
5. Who took the box was anybody's guess.
6. For days Rex gave us a superior look whenever he saw us.
7. It was a look that said, "I told you so."
8. When in Rome, do as the Romans do.
9. I returned the letters we received to the person who had sent them.
10. Whoso would be a man must be a non-conformist.
11. I thank you for what you did for me when I was ill.
12. People who say "I feel BADLY" do not realize that "feel" is a linking verb and that it should be completed by "bad," which is a predicate adjective.
13. "I feel badly" means "My sense of touch is defective."
14. Above the Arctic Circle, life requires that you stay alert.
15. What I like about Roy is his great sense of humor.
16. If he calls, tell him I am out.
17. Ned and Elmer have decided that, if it rains, they will not go to the picnic.
18. He jests at scars who never felt a wound.
19. He who laughs last laughs best.
20. Because he ran away before the circus came to town, he missed the ad which offered jobs to whoever could swing a hammer.

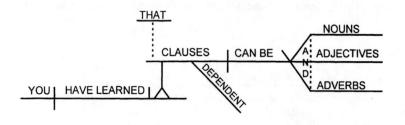

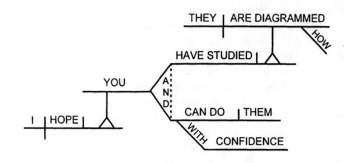

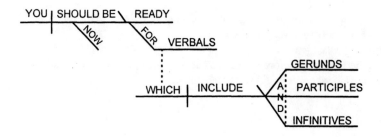

CHAPTER FIVE
VERBALS

Memorize this definition:

A VERBAL is a VERB FORM used as ANOTHER PART OF SPEECH.

You have just seen how a NOUN JOB can be done by a whole clause. You have also seen how a whole clause could serve as an ADJECTIVE or ADVERB. Our clever language has another device to expand and pep up NOUNS, ADJECTIVES, and ADVERBS. It is the VERBAL.

There are three kinds of VERBALS:
                         —GERUNDS-----------always nouns
                         —PARTICIPLES-------always adjectives
                         —INFINITIVES-------nouns, adjectives, or adverbs

5-A. GERUNDS

Gerunds are the easiest verbal to learn, so we will start with them. With gerunds, you can always count on two things:

A GERUND ALWAYS ENDS IN **-ING**
A GERUND IS ALWAYS A **NOUN**

If you were asked to diagram "Swimming is fun," you would no doubt say to yourself, " 'Swimming' is the subject." Of course it is. So you would diagram it:

But now you are ready to examine the "verbness" of "swimming." It has been made out of the verb "to swim." It is the name (as all nouns are names) of an ACTION (for "to swim" is a verb of action.)

WHEN THE **-ING** FORM OF A VERB IS USED AS A NOUN, IT IS A GERUND.

You can immediately name many activities as gerunds: reading, dancing, running, sleeping, even BEING.

There is a special way GERUNDS are diagrammed to show their "verbness." At first it may seem silly, but wait till you see all the verb tricks a GERUND can do, and then you will see the necessity for its special treatment.

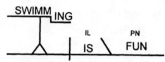

Before we examine all the verb things a GERUND can do, let us observe the noun things. (I suppose the reason for the broken horizontal line is to show that the gerund is part noun, part verb. Both nouns and verbs sit on horizontal lines.) We have already said that in "Swimming is fun" the gerund "swimming" was acting as subject. That's one noun job gerunds can do.

Exercise 5-1: Diagram these and discover for yourself what other noun jobs gerunds may perform.

1. My hobby is swimming.
2. I like swimming.
3. I am interested in swimming.
4. I give swimming all my time.

You should have been able to find a gerund PN, DO, OP and IO. Check the answers to see if you diagrammed them correctly. You should have!

So much for the "noun-ness" of GERUNDS. How much "verbness" do they still have? Well, what can verbs do?

1) Various verbs can take PA, PN or DO COMPLEMENTS.
2) Verbs are modified by ADVERBS.
3) Verbs have SUBJECTS.

Could GERUNDS have COMPLEMENTS?

Swimming the English Channel is dangerous.
Being king is a responsibility.
Staying happy was a challenge.

Let's see how they are diagrammed:

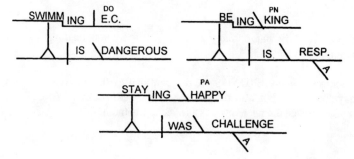

Even though the GERUNDS above, "swimming," "being," and "staying," had enough "nounness" to be subjects, they proved that GERUNDS have enough "verbness" to take the verb COMPLEMENTS, DO, PN, and PA.

How about ADVERBIAL MODIFIERS of GERUNDS? Could you say "swimming against the current," "actually being king," or "staying happy under those conditions"? Yes.

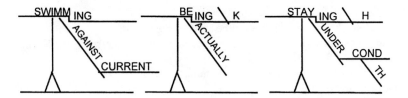

The expressions "against the current," "actually," and "under those conditions" tell HOW the verb was carried out. So GERUNDS can have ADVERBIAL MODIFIERS.

Finally, can GERUNDS have SUBJECTS?

Well, sort of. What is a subject? The "doer or be-er" of the verb. Take a look at this:

Singing won a prize.

We want to know WHOSE singing. Who DID the singing?
NELLIE'S singing won a prize.

Here is an interesting rule:
THE "SUBJECT" OF A GERUND IS IN THE POSSESSIVE CASE.

That means we don't say "Nellie singing won a prize." We make "Nellie" possessive: "Nellie's."

Notice these examples of "subjects" of gerunds:

I like Mike's dancing. His going will not make us happy. I am curious about your growing vegetables in water.

We speak of the "subject" of a gerund in quotes because after all a gerund is a noun, not a real verb. Remember the definition of a CLAUSE: a group of words with a SUBJECT and a VERB. If "Nellie's singing" were a real subject and verb, we would call it a "gerund clause." But since "Nellie's" REALLY is telling "WHOSE" about a NOUN, we say that it is a GERUND PHRASE.

A VERBAL AND THE WORDS THAT GO WITH IT MAKE A **PHRASE**, NOT A CLAUSE.

Of course, a verbal can occur without any other words, as in our original "Swimming is fun" sentence.

Exercise 5-2: Diagram these sentences, which include gerunds and gerund phrases.

1. In the summer Margie enjoys canning tomatoes.
2. Ron's partying has resulted in his mother's worrying about him.
3. At the beginning of winter, skiing became more popular than hiking. (Remember "than"?)
4. His thinking was that the producer would turn to directing.
5. Seeing is believing.
6. Through all the arguing, Mary's knitting was never abandoned.
7. Misery is finding a dent in the fender of your new car.
8. Reaching the top is easier than staying there.
9. He lost interest in rowing and gave flying his attention.
10. Ed's cooking has improved since he began reading those recipes.

The answers should straighten out any problems. Before we leave these easy gerunds, though, we should remember that NOT EVERYTHING ending in -ING is a gerund. Some plain old verbs end in -ing. To make this point clearer:

Molly is baking pies. Her hobby is baking pies.

"Molly" DOES NOT EQUAL "baking."
"Hobby" DOES EQUAL "baking."

So make certain that an **-ing** word is really acting as a noun before you call it a gerund.

As we have seen, these **-ing** words can be VERBS and GERUNDS. Alas, they can also be something else:

5-B. PARTICIPLES

Participles are almost as easy as gerunds. But not quite.

—PARTICIPLES ARE ALWAYS ADJECTIVES.
—<u>PRESENT</u> PARTICIPLES END IN -ING.
—<u>PAST</u> PARTICIPLES END IN -D, -T, or -N.

Examine these two sentences:

> They ran to the house that was burning.
> They ran to the burning house.

In the first sentence, the adjective clause, "that was burning," modifies house. It answers "Which one?" In the second sentence, the PARTICIPLE "burning" modifies "house." In this case the PARTICIPLE is in front of the noun it modifies, like ordinary adjectives. Here is the diagram:

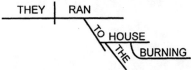

The line for participles has an "elbow" in it between the slant for adjective and the horizontal line for verb, since a PARTICIPLE is an ADJECTIVE made out of a VERB.

Let us look at a past participle:

> The burned child fears the fire.

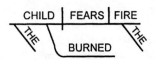

Exercise 5-3: Here are some easy sentences with participles. Diagram them.

1. A rolling stone gathers no moss.
2. The shifting sands of time cause changed circumstances.
3. The determined boy made a hook with a bent pin.
4. Discouraged, he sat by the dying embers.
5. A worried gardener looked at the wilting plants.

Check the answers to see how you did on your first participles. These were quite easy. You knew participles would get worse. You may even have guessed how.

If PARTICIPLES have "verbness" in them (and they do), they will do verb things. For instance, let us take:

> He looked at the wilting plants.

Suppose we say:

He looked at the plants wilting in the sun.

"In the sun" tells "where" they were wilting. So:

PARTICIPLES CAN TAKE ADVERBIAL MODIFIERS.

This makes sense, since, after all, a PARTICIPLE is an ADJECTIVE, and adverbs modify adjectives.

Notice that when the participle, "wilting," got a modifier, it moved to a new position AFTER the noun it modified. Here are some sentences with participles that have adverbial modifiers. As you diagram them, notice the word order.

Exercise 5-4:

1. Soaked by the rain, Rex howled at the door.
2. Father, defeated at checkers, tried chess.
3. The tree surgeon looked at the oak, eaten out with rot.
4. Linda, crying dismally over her broken doll, did not see the newly-arrived package.
5. The sailor, exhausted by his night of duty, rowed the passengers toward their eagerly waiting relatives.

How were those? There are several things to discuss before we leave this exercise. Look at Sentence 1. The PARTICIPIAL PHRASE (the participle and any words that go with it) begins the sentence. It is followed by a comma. There is a comma rule that says, "An introductory participial phrase is followed by a comma."

Look again at that phrase and the word that follows:

Soaked by the rain, Rex...

Another rule says:

AN INTRODUCTORY PARTICIPIAL PHRASE MUST MODIFY THE VERY NEXT NOUN IN THE SENTENCE.

Otherwise, it is a

D*A*N*G*L*I*N*G
P*A*R*T*I*C*I*P*L*E
(A   V*E*R*Y   B*A*D   T*H*I*N*G)

Let me give you an example:

Running down the street, his shoelaces came untied.
Do you see those shoelaces jogging down the street all by themselves? That's what the sentence says. Here is another good one:

Hanging over the side of the ship, his eye was caught by a piece of rope.

There goes that eye, like a fried egg or one of Dali's watches!

One more thing: the "newly-arrived package." Notice the hyphen. When an adverb modifies a participle that is in front of its noun, a hyphen often separates the adverb and participle: freshly-baked bread, plainly-dressed woman, recently-bereaved widow, etc.
Sometimes a noun or adjective will modify a participle in this way: home-grown corn, smoke-cured ham, new-born baby, old-fashioned goodness, etc.
There is a very confusing thing about some participles. Remember that sometimes ADJECTIVES are PREDICATE ADJECTIVES.

She was enchanted by his accent.

How can you tell whether the sentence is

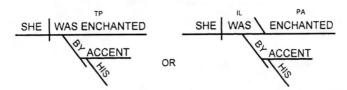

The answer is, you can't always be sure. You must decide whether the subject is really receiving an action (TP) or the past participle is describing a condition (PA). People will disagree about a given sentence. I lean toward TP in the sentence above.

We have seen participles show their "verbness" by having adverbial modifiers. What other verb traits could participles have?
Raking the lawn, Tom found a dollar.   Being honest, he returned it.
Becoming a butterfly, the little creature grew beautiful.

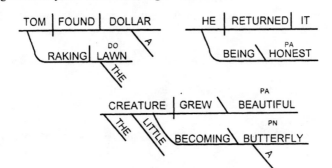

Sure enough, participles CAN have COMPLEMENTS, just like real verbs.

Real verbs have subjects. Even gerunds have "subjects." What could be the subject of a participle? Look at the sentences above. What or who <u>did</u> the "raking" and "being" and "becoming"? Why, "Tom," "he," and "creature," the NOUNS the participles MODIFY. So, unlike gerunds, participles will not have a special rule about "subjects."

EXCEPT: NOMINATIVE ABSOLUTE

One rather unusual construction is the NOMINATIVE ABSOLUTE. You MAY find a sentence in which the participle has its own "subject" and the whole participial phrase seems to stand by itself. For instance:

The work having been finished, the men moved on.

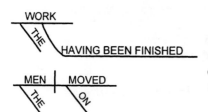

The NOMINATIVE ABSOLUTE has NO grammatical connection with the sentence and is diagrammed like an interjection above the subject.

Gerunds don't have any HELPING VERBS. Participles may.

Tom, raking the lawn, <u>having</u> raked the lawn, <u>having been</u> raking the lawn. The girl, thrown from the horse, <u>being</u> thrown, <u>having been</u> thrown, etc.

Before diagramming some sentences with all kinds of participial phrases, let's see how really loaded down a participial phrase might be:

Tom, DILIGENTLY RAKING HIS UNCLE'S WEEDY LAWN WITH RENEWED ENTHUSIASM BECAUSE HE HAD HEARD THAT SOMEONE HAD WALKED ACROSS THE GRASS WITH A HOLE IN HIS POCKET, found a dollar.

That's not a well-constructed sentence, but it is technically correct. Any of you Superstars want to diagram it just for fun? OK, check the answers, 5-X.

Exercise 5-5: Diagram these sensible sentences. (There are 12 participles, I think.)

1. Taking a lunch break, Jill opened her plastic-wrapped sandwich.
2. She ate a devilled egg, drank a malted milk, and watched the people hurrying back to the office.
3. Having remained quiet for so long, Jim surprised us with his startling remarks.

4. Having been defeated in the contest, the runner, panting for breath, threw himself on the ground.
5. Ann, seeing her chance, helped herself to a fattening plate of fried potatoes.

If you were able to manage the last exercise, you are now ready to meet some sentences with MIXED gerunds and participles. Remember that GERUNDS are NOUNS, PARTICIPLES are ADJECTIVES!

Exercise 5-6:

1. Stepping on the boat, Jo glanced uneasily toward the lifeboats hanging over the side.
2. She liked sailing but she was afraid of falling into the churning water.
3. Troubled by the number of dying trees, the farmer began examining the insects infesting the branches.
4. Swimming faster, Harry neared the screaming child.
5. After grabbing it by the hair, he pulled toward shore, arriving just above the roaring falls.

Before we leave participles, we should look at a troubling thing about some of them. As ADJECTIVES, they SHOULD stick to answering the adjective questions about nouns. BUT frequently they seem to be telling "where" or "how." Look at this:

I saw him <u>walking toward town</u>.

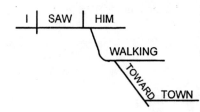

The "walking toward town" really tells "where" you saw him, if indeed "him" was the person doing the walking. Notice that this particular phrase might be interpreted as "while I was walking."

PARTICIPLES ARE STRANGE!

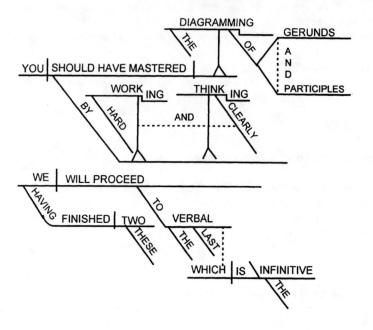

5-C. INFINITIVES

Do you recall that you read (many pages ago) that the INFINITIVE form of the verb is the form used with TO? Examples: to think, to be, to run, to build, etc.

Why is this form called the INFINITIVE? What word do you think of? "Infinite." Something that is infinite is not limited. It can go on and on. An INFINITIVE verb is in many ways free. In the infinitive "to see," we don't know:

—WHO IS DOING THE SEEING
—HOW MANY ARE SEEING
—WHEN THE SEEING IS/WAS DONE

In addition to being the BASIC FORM (the one you look up in the dictionary) of a verb, an INFINITIVE is also a VERBAL. It can be a NOUN, ADJECTIVE, or ADVERB.

Think of a sentence with an infinitive in it. Probably you made up one with the infinitive used as a NOUN. Was it like these?

1. I like to swim.
2. I want to see him.

3. To err is human.
4. To dance is to live.

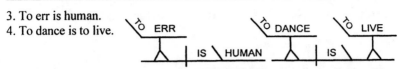

Number 2 showed you that INFINITIVES can have DO's. You can immediately (I hope) test out whether infinitives can have PA's and PN's.

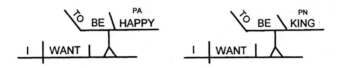

Can INFINITIVES have adverbial modifiers like real verbs? Gerunds and participles can. So can INFINITIVES.

I like to swim <u>in the pool</u>. (where)   I like to swim <u>lazily</u>. (how)
I like to swim <u>for exercise</u>. (why)   I like to swim <u>at night</u>. (when)

So far we have learned that INFINITIVES can have COMPLEMENTS and ADVERBIAL MODIFIERS. What about SUBJECTS?

He wants to swim.   He wants ME to swim.
They asked to sing.   They asked HIM to sing.

The first sentence of each pair indicates that the action of the infinitive is to be done by the subject. The second sentences of each pair are quite different. The "ME" and "HIM" are to do the action of the infinitive.

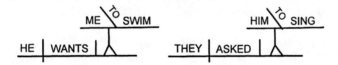

An interesting thing about the "ME" and "HIM" is their CASE. Remember CASE? Nominative, Objective, Possessive? Nominative, you were told, is for SUBJECTS and PREDICATE NOMINATIVES. But NOT for "subjects" of INFINITIVES!

THE "SUBJECT" OF AN INFINITIVE IS IN THE OBJECTIVE CASE.

(This rule is similar to: "The 'subject' of a gerund is in the possessive case.")

We must also explore INFINITIVES as ADJECTIVES and ADVERBS.

1. The book to read is *True Grit*.
2. I came to help.

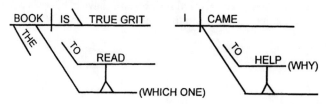

Exercise 5-7: Here are some sentences with infinitives. Diagram them, remembering that infinitives have complements, adverbs, and sometimes "subjects."

1. I asked him to forgive me.
2. Why do you want to do a parachute jump?
3. He was looking for a movie to see with his grandma.
4. They ordered us to park here.
5. This is the way to paint fences.
6. Some people do not have the sense to come in out of the rain.
7. We hold these truths to be self-evident.
8. To see the fireworks we had to climb onto the roof.
9. I am going to see why they asked him to stop singing.
10. He is able to decide things for himself.

In Sentence 9, "to see" can be interpreted as "why" the "I" is doing the "going," but we really use the expression "going to" to indicate future action.

There is one more tricky thing about infinitives. They were so nice, weren't they? You just looked for "to" followed by a verb and figured out what it was doing. Well, take a look at this:

I saw him take the cookies.

Certain verbs, such as **see, let,** and **make,** may be followed by infinitive constructions which have a "subject" followed by an infinitive WITHOUT the "to." Examples:

They let him go. We made him wait.

Exercise 5-8: Now we have covered ALL THE VERBALS! Polish your new skills by diagramming these sentences, which include gerunds, participles, and infinitives.

1. Running down the street, he started panting.
2. Jogging had been his hobby for only two days.
3. Rex, straining at his leash, wanted to go along.
4. To move all your things to another place would be costly.
5. Giving his all to overcome the snarling dragon, he advanced toward the cave.
6. He began to speak about the worsening crisis.
7. Suddenly everyone heard a creaking of the timbers.
8. Running for cover as the roof began to cave in, the audience agreed on the need for improving things.
9. Why did he hope to find an honest man among those twisted cynics?
10 Having been fed on pureed vegetables and unseasoned meats, the baby was surprised by its first bite of pizza.

If you managed to do that exercise well, you are nearly ready to graduate into the free-for-all of sentences as they are written and spoken. With only a few more constructions, you will be ready to diagram—oh, the Declaration of Independence, if that seems like a good thing to do.

You should have discovered that sometimes our grammatical construction does not exactly coincide with our meaning, but nearly always there is a logical pattern to our sentences, even the ones we toss off carelessly in speech. Now that you understand the basic framework of the sentence, you can use this knowledge to improve your own sentences and English usage.

I have never been able to understand how a student was to use "stronger" verbs until he knew what a verb was, or how he could "vary his sentence structure" before he had seen how main and subordinate clauses differed, or how he could "avoid dangling participles" without knowing what a participle was supposed to look like when it **wasn't** dangling. Diagramming provides a systematic, clear, interesting method to understand and use our great language.

CHAPTER SIX
ADDITIONAL CONSTRUCTIONS

There are three fairly important constructions which have not been mentioned so far:

—APPOSITIVE
—OBJECTIVE COMPLEMENT
—ADVERBIAL NOUN

You may already know them and may have been wondering what had become of them. The reason they were not included earlier is that when it was logical to introduce them, there was so much else to cover, it seemed just too much at the time. So here they are now.

You have learned that NOUNS can do quite a few jobs:

1) SUBJECT   (**REX** barks.)
2) DIRECT OBJECT   (I see **REX**.)
3) PREDICATE NOMINATIVE   (Rex is a **DOG**.)
4) OBJECT OF A PREPOSITION   (I yelled at **REX**.)
5) INDIRECT OBJECT   (I gave **REX** a bone.)
6) DIRECT ADDRESS   (**REX**, you come here.)
7) RETAINED OBJECT   (Rex was given a **BONE**.)

The three new constructions named above are also NOUN JOBS.

6-A. APPOSITIVE

An APPOSITIVE is a NOUN (and any modifiers) that RESTATES ANOTHER NOUN and SHARES ITS CONSTRUCTION.

That is a rather deadly definition, isn't it? Examples will help:

My friend, Ann Doe, has a car.

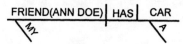

The APPOSITIVE goes in parentheses beside the word with which it is "in apposition."

The wicked witch, the one with the wart on her nose, was defeated.

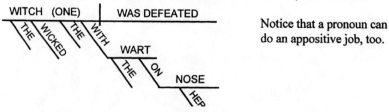

Notice that a pronoun can do an appositive job, too.

Exercise 6-1: Diagram these sentences with appositives:

1. Nora, the girl with the big smile, was waving at Jim.
2. My sister Nancy gave a present, a big Barbie doll, to her friend Sara on her birthday, July 20.
3. Rex, the wonderdog, dashed to the rescue of Tabby, the cat.
4. You, the voters of tomorrow, will have to solve these problems: overpopulation, pollution, and hunger.
5. William the Conqueror brought French influence to England, an Anglo-Saxon land.

You may have noticed that some appositives and appositive phrases (the noun and words that go with it) are set off by commas and some are not. Very closely associated appositives and those that are essential to the identification of the noun are not always set off by commas. But if an appositive has a comma in front of it, it must have one after it (unless it is followed by another mark of punctuation.) Example:

My sister Mabel is pretty.

OR

My sister, Mabel, is pretty.

In Sentence 4 you found a colon (:) preceding a list. The nouns in the list are in apposition with the preceding noun, in this case "problems," and share its construction, here acting as direct object of "to solve."

Appositives can be verbals and even occasionally noun clauses. Observe these examples:

His dream, to go over Niagara Falls in a barrel, is unsound.
His dream, that he can go over Niagara Falls in a barrel, is unsound.

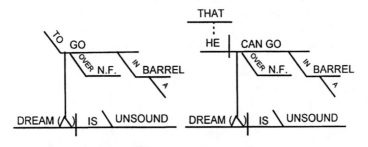

6-B. OBJECTIVE COMPLEMENT

They named the baby Bill.   They called the dog Rex.

	TA	DO	OC		TA	DO	OC
THEY	NAMED	BABY	BILL	THEY	CALLED	DOG	REX

We thought that he was handsome.   We thought him handsome.

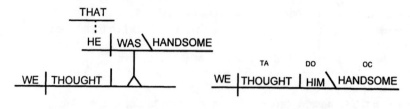

We chose him to be president.   We chose him president.

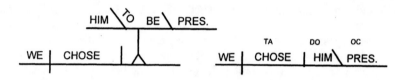

Study the diagrams above carefully. In every case the MAIN verb in the sentence is TRANSITIVE ACTIVE, requiring a DIRECT OBJECT. In the sentences with OC (OBJECTIVE COMPLEMENT), the direct object is completed by either a noun or an adjective.

CERTAIN VERBS OF NAMING, THINKING, OR SELECTING MAY HAVE THE DIRECT OBJECT COMPLETED BY A NOUN OR ADJECTIVE CALLED AN OBJECTIVE COMPLEMENT.

Notice that you could take each DO-OC pair and make a kind of linking verb statement:
        "baby is Bill,"   "dog is Rex,"   "he is handsome," etc.

Exercise 6-2: Diagram these sentences to get practice with OBJECTIVE COMPLEMENTS.

1. They called her "Frivolous Sal."
2. Melvin considers you his friend.
3. Should they have elected Herman a director of the company?
4. The doctor finally pronounced him able to travel.
5. The captain had already chosen Bill first mate.

6-C. ADVERBIAL NOUN

By now if you don't know that adverbs answer the questions "where, when, why, and how," you just haven't been trying. You have surely noticed that sometimes it is hard to know exactly which adverbial question is being answered.

Sometimes "how" means "to what degree" or "under what circumstances," or even "despite what circumstances" (i.e., an "although" clause). But you have developed, I hope, an ADVERB SENSE - an awareness that a certain word or expression is modifying a verb, adjective or other adverb.

So far you have seen the following ADVERB CONSTRUCTIONS:

He came SUDDENLY.   (single adverb)
He came IN A BUS.   (prepositional phrase)
He came WHEN I CALLED.   (adverb clause)
He came TO HELP.   (infinitive)

You have not been confronted (at least not intentionally) with these constructions:

I waited three years.   He ran ten yards.

You might immediately think that "years" is the direct object of "waited" After all, "Waited what?" "Three years." But THINK. "Waited" is really, in this usage INtransitive. And the sentence might just as well read, "I waited FOR three years."

Here "years" is an ADVERBIAL NOUN, modified by the ADJECTIVE "three."

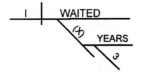
The ADVERBIAL NOUN is diagrammed like the indirect object.

The second example, "He ran ten yards," is a little different. You might make a case that sometimes "run" is transitive with a distance as the direct object: "He ran the mile in five minutes." Here "mile" would be the DO of "ran."

But since we can say just as well, "He ran FOR ten yards," surely "ten yards" answers "how" in the sense of "how far."

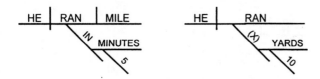

What about "yesterday" and "today"? My dictionary says they are both nouns AND adverbs. So it is all right to diagram them as adverbs when they answer "when."

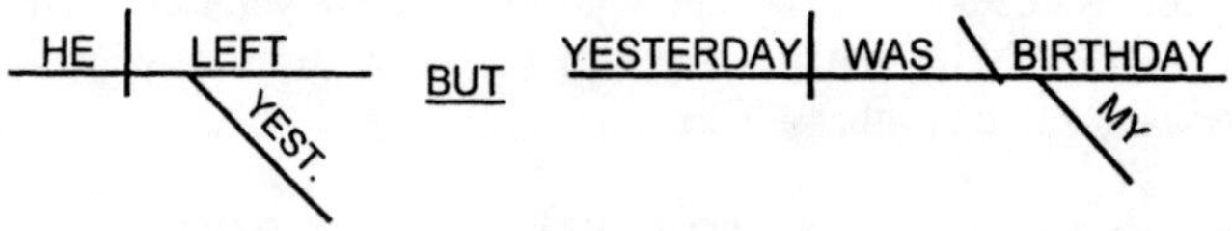

But the days of the week are nouns.

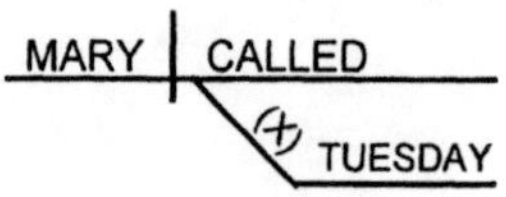

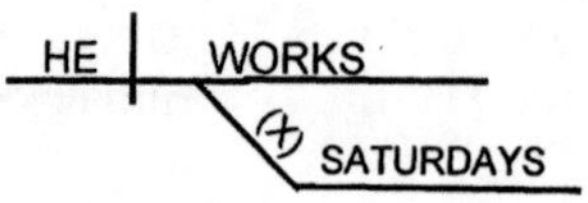

And don't forget good old

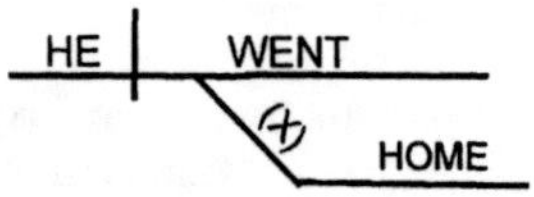

If you enjoy puzzling over such things, consider the grammatical uses of money. The dictionary definition of "cost" is hard to figure out (look it up for yourself), but I suspect you can think of

"It cost three dollars"

as   or

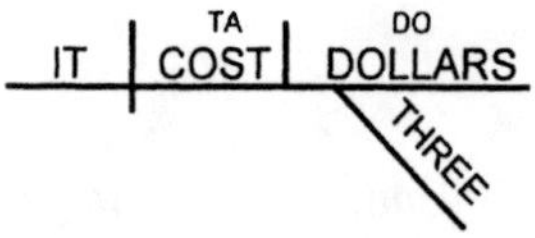

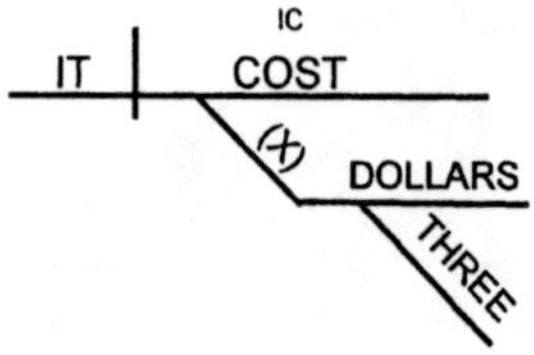

However, what about this one:

It is worth three dollars.

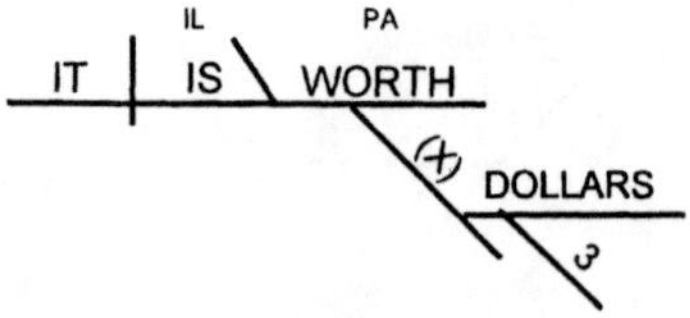

I'm not at all sure that "dollars" is an adverbial noun. I think perhaps "worth" is a special case.

A similar construction might be:

I am aware that he lied.

If we said, "I know that he lied," we would diagram it:

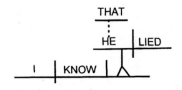

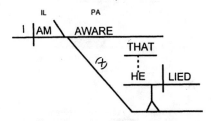

BUT ___ won't TAKE a NOUN CLAUSE AS OBJECT.

HOWEVER, maybe "that he lied" could be an ADVERBIAL NOUN telling "how" "I am aware." Thus:

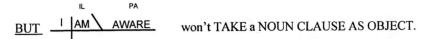

Exercise 6-3: Diagram these sentences, being on the lookout for whatever you think might be an ADVERBIAL NOUN.

1. He will leave today or Tuesday.
2. He ran three miles, ate four sandwiches, and went home.
3. Last night the concert seemed to last hours.
4. Nellie and Bob are going fishing.
5. He spent three years researching that book.

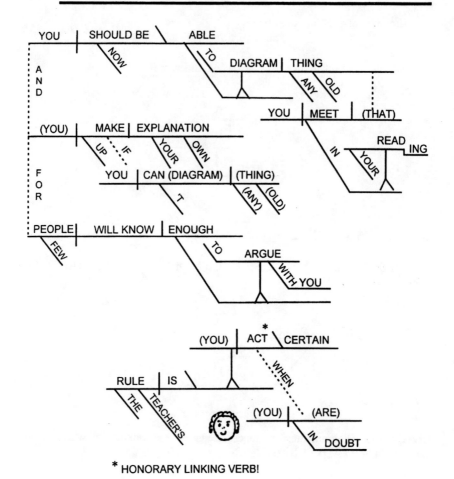

* HONORARY LINKING VERB!

CHAPTER SEVEN
COMPOUND AND COMPLEX SENTENCES

If you have studied everything in the book so far, you will have only to learn the names of the constructions which you have already practiced.

Sentences are sometimes classified by the number and kinds of clauses they contain.

1. SIMPLE SENTENCE—contains <u>one</u> MAIN (or independent) CLAUSE
2. COMPOUND SENTENCE—contains <u>two</u> or <u>more</u> MAIN CLAUSES
3. COMPLEX SENTENCE—contains <u>one</u> MAIN and <u>one</u> or <u>more</u> SUBORDINATE (or dependent) CLAUSES
4. COMPOUND-COMPLEX SENTENCE—contains <u>two</u> or <u>more</u> MAIN CLAUSES and <u>one</u> or <u>more</u> SUBORDINATE CLAUSES

Every sentence MUST have at least one main clause, of course, or it is not a sentence. The first sentences you diagrammed were all SIMPLE sentences. Then when you studied "Compound Elements," you saw that two main clauses might be joined to make a COMPOUND sentence:

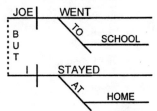

As soon as you diagrammed your first dependent clause, you had diagrammed a COMPLEX sentence Additional subordinate clauses would not make it any more "complex."

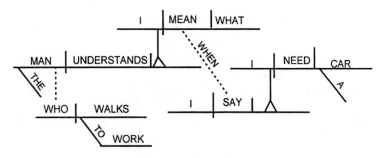

Finally, putting together the requirements for compound and complex, we have a COMPOUND-COMPLEX sentence:

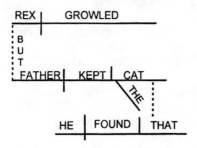

Could it be simpler or more logical?

Exercise 7-1: Diagram these and tell which category each is.

1. John is mad and I am glad and I know how to please him.
2. This is the cat that killed the rat that ate the malt that lay in the house that Jack built.
3. The sun, shining across the bay with an unmatched splendor, scattered its rays upon the tiny sailboats lying at anchor in the shallows.
4. I bought one; you will be sorry if you do.
5. I do what I should not do, but I do not do what I should.

There. Any surprises in the answers?

CHAPTER EIGHT
MISCELLANY

This section includes all the "leftovers" that I would be uneasy about omitting. Some items cover special cases of diagramming but others deal with usage matters which can be made particularly clear through diagrams. Since diagramming is a MEANS to understanding our language and using it well, this book should at least start you in the direction of better usage.

8-A. ABOUT ADJECTIVE CLAUSES

1. Avoid the "INDEFINITE WHICH."

It rained, which made us cancel our picnic.

OK,   IT | RAINED   but from what do you HANG the relative pronoun?

He was really very angry, which frightened me.

Same problem. It wasn't the "he" which frightened me, nor the "was," nor the "angry."

Both of the "which" clauses above are examples of ADJECTIVE CLAUSES TRYING TO FIND A NOUN OR PRONOUN TO MODIFY, but ending up trying to modify a whole sentence. The best antidote is to rewrite the sentence completely:

We canceled our picnic because it rained.
He was so angry that we were frightened.

WHICH MUST MODIFY A SPECIFIC NOUN CONSTRUCTION, NOT A WHOLE CLAUSE!

(When you write a sentence with "which," be sure that you have a place to "hang" it.)

?·······~~~·······⟨WHICH⟩

2. "WHERE" and "WHEN" can sometimes be RELATIVE PRONOUNS.

Remember your list of relative pronouns: WHO, WHOSE, WHOM, THAT, WHICH. Well, once in a while we tell "which one" by telling "where" or "when."

Observe:

I know the house where he was born.
Remember the time when he sang.

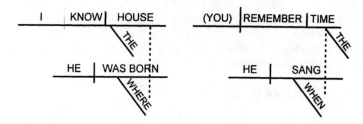

8-B. ABOUT ADVERB CLAUSES

1. LIKE is a PREPOSITION, NOT a SUBORDINATING CONJUNCTION.

There used to be an advertisement which would be diagrammed like this:

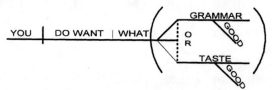

Apparently enough English teachers used it as a hideous example that the company thought to capitalize on the public's general resentment of people who try to raise the cultural level (English teachers). So they came out with another slogan diagrammed below:

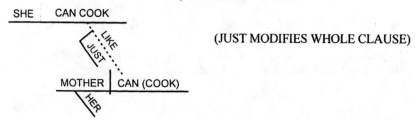

The basic problem is that we seem to NEED a conjunction that "feels better" than "as" in certain comparisons. It is technically poor usage to say,

She can cook just like her mother can.

(JUST MODIFIES WHOLE CLAUSE)

Putting the verb "can" in there makes "like" a conjunction. Yet even an English teacher wouldn't say, "She can cook just as her mother can." Ugh! One solution is to leave out the "can" and make "mother" the object of the preposition "like."

Changing usage may solve the problem. When enough educated people accept "like" as a conjunction, the rest of us peasants will not be sneered at for using it in formal situations. But despite the limpness of the warnings in our ever more permissive dictionaries, "LIKE" as a CONJUNCTION ain't arrived yet.

2. "SO. . .THAT" acts as a SUBORDINATING CONJUNCTION.

Usually "that" clauses are adjective or noun clauses:

This is the book that was lost. (ADJ.)
The truth is that it was stolen. (NOUN)

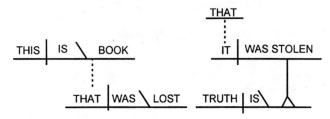

But look at these:

He is <u>so</u> thin <u>that</u> you cannot see him.
The bird flew <u>so</u> quickly <u>that</u> I missed it.

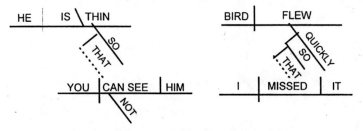

3. The SUBJUNCTIVE MOOD is still alive, but barely.

School children used to be taught about MOOD:

INDICATIVE—makes a declarative statement
INTERROGATIVE—asks a question (I was taught that, but it's not in my dictionary now.)
IMPERATIVE—gives a command

SUBJUNCTIVE—expresses a condition contrary to fact or a wish

If you want to know more about the subjunctive mood in all its elegant variety, get a very old grammar book and look it up. It sounds so pretty! But in today's usage one of the few places where the subjunctive is alive and well is in "if" clauses that are CONTRARY TO FACT, especially in the FIRST PERSON SINGULAR (I):

> If I **were** you (but of course I'm NOT you)
> If I **were** rich (alas, that's contrary to fact, too)

The other place where the subjunctive mood is different from the indicative is in the THIRD person singular:

> If he or she or it **were** honest (but they aren't)

One more situation for this mood: the noun clause after "I wish."

I wish that I were you.

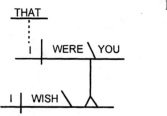

This is all the subjunctive we have space for, but be on the lookout in old-fashioned writing for such things as "were he to go" or "if he be sent." SUBJUNCTIVE!

8-C. ABOUT PRONOUNS

There are so many kinds of pronouns that you will need to consult another source to track them all down. There are DEMONSTRATIVE, INTERROGATIVE, RELATIVE (your old friends), REFLEXIVE, INTENSIVE, INDEFINITE, PERSONAL, and more.

Remember how we sorted out WHO and WHOM? If you don't, look back to adjective clauses and relative pronouns in Chapter 4. The basic rule was that the CASE depended on the use of WHO or WHOM in its own clause. There is another group of pronouns that give trouble, and the easiest way to sort them out is in a chart:

PERSONAL PRONOUNS

Singular	Nominative	Objective	Possessive
1st Person	I	me	my, mine
2nd Person	you	you	your, yours
3rd Person	he, she, it	him, her, it	his, her, hers, its

Plural			
1st Person	we	us	our, ours
2nd Person	you	you	your, yours
3rd Person	they	them	their, theirs

If you haven't learned this chart already, learn it now. These are terms with which you should be familiar, especially in studying foreign languages.

Now that you know when to use the NOMINATIVE CASE (SUBJECTS and PREDICATE NOMINATIVES, of course) and the OBJECTIVE CASE (OBJECTS of all kinds and "SUBJECTS" of infinitives), you should have no trouble understanding why these forms are chosen by what contemporary grammar books call "careful writers and speakers":

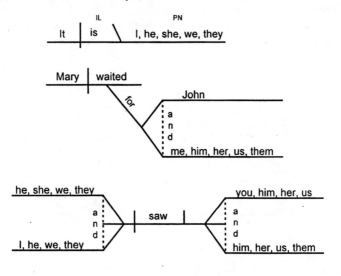

In speech, the form "It is me" has gained considerable acceptance among the educated. Perhaps it seems somehow more "objective" about oneself. (Ha ha!) But the other persons should stay nominative in the PREDICATE NOMINATIVE.

While we are on the subject of usage as accepted by educated speakers or writers (what used to be called CORRECT as opposed to INCORRECT in the bad old days), there are social classes of what **I** am going to call ERRORS. Picture the different social levels of the people who make the following **errors:**

> Me and him were fighting.
> He's waiting for you and I.

Both sentences contain wrong PRONOUN CASES. I certainly hope you were able to find them. I have tried to figure out why the NOMINATIVE case is misused by the GENTEEL and the OBJECTIVE case by the TOUGH GUYS. I simply don't know. But I wish I had a nickel for every time I have heard a college graduate say:

> between you and **I**,   for **she** and Bob,   to Mabel and **I**,
> AND MORE BAD STUFF LIKE THAT.

Presumably, if you have worked your way this far through the book, you are beyond using the OBJECTIVE case as SUBJECT ("Me and her went. . .") though maybe you are not above using OBJECTIVE as PREDICATE NOMINATIVE (It was them. . ."). However, you **may** be one of those dear earnest souls who feel they MUST put the second pronoun of a COMPOUND <u>OBJECT</u> into the NOMINATIVE CASE. "It sounds so much <u>better</u>," you say. Well, work on it until it <u>doesn't</u> sound better. Say these over and over till they feel natural:

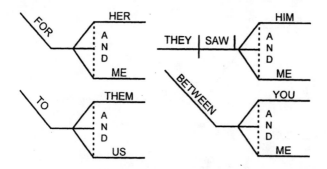

Another place where diagramming will help you understand proper CASE comes after the contraction "Let's."

"Let's" means "let us." Who is to do the letting? Understood "you."

Examine this sentence:

Let's go to the store.

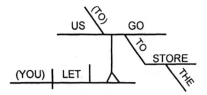

Notice that the "'s" or "us" becomes the "SUBJECT" of the infinitive "go," and "subjects" of infinitives are in the OBJECTIVE CASE. Sure enough, your chart will show that "us" is indeed OBJECTIVE.

Now, suppose I want to emphasize the people included in that "us": second person singular and first person singular.

Let's _____ and _____ go to the store.

The blanks will be APPOSITIVES (remember them?) and will SHARE THE CONSTRUCTION of the thing with which they are in apposition. (Whew! Am I glad I can diagram it for you!)

Because "you" and "me" are in apposition with "us," they take the same CASE as "us," OBJECTIVE.

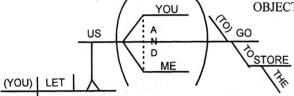

After all of that, you may wish to give thanks that our dear English language has CASE differences only for PERSONAL PRONOUNS and WHO.

8-D. ABOUT PREPOSITIONAL PHRASES

1. Some PREPOSITIONS have TWO WORDS.
   Examples: because of, instead of, according to, etc.
   Diagram them as one word.

2. Some lists of PREPOSITIONS give some THREE-WORD ones.
   Examples: in front of, in spite of, by means of
   I think of these as really one and a half prepositional phrases and diagram them:

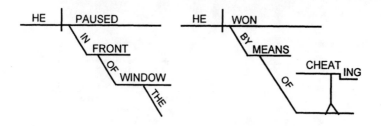

3. While PREPOSITIONAL PHRASES are normally ADJECTIVES and ADVERBS, sometimes they do strange things. Observe:

Over the fence is out.

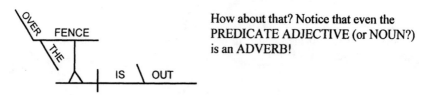

How about that? Notice that even the PREDICATE ADJECTIVE (or NOUN?) is an ADVERB!

With the fingers is the best way to eat bacon.

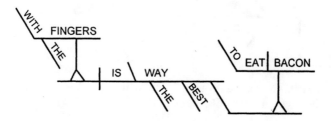

In the last sentence you may feel that "way" should be the subject. But that leaves "with the fingers" as PREDICATE NOUN, or something.

We have earlier mentioned how "to be" verbs seem to be COMPLETED rather than MODIFIED by prepositional phrases:

She was in the barn.   The appointment had been for three.

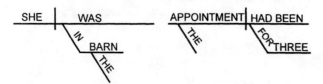

These "exceptions" just make you stay on your toes and appreciate the flexibility of our language.

8-E. ABOUT NOUNS

WORDS THAT NAME THINGS—NOUNS—ARE WILLING TO WORK ALMOST ANYWHERE.

1. Many NOUNS also work as VERBS. Of course, deciding whether the NOUN "hammer" came before or after the VERB "to hammer" is like worrying over the old "chicken-egg" controversy. But many words used as VERBS also name objects. Examples:

> They tabled the motion.   (put it on the **table** to delay it)
> He was floored by the suggestion.   (knocked to the **floor**)
> Were you booked for the crime? (name written in the record **books**)
> The dog treed the possum. (chased him up a **tree**)

Notice the vividness and strength these verbs have because you can picture the objects in the scene.

2. NOUNS often serve as ADJECTIVES.

> Look at the hat.
> Which one? The BEAVER hat.
> What kind? A FELT hat.
> Whose? GEORGE's hat.

Possession usually requires the "apostrophe-s" form. But we sometimes say "an Edison invention," "a Renoir painting," etc., showing "whose" as well as "what kind."

3. The ADVERBIAL NOUN has its own section in Chapter 6. But you remember it, don't you?

He waited three hours.

WELL! I have not covered every situation you will find. For instance, the subtitle of <u>REX BARKS</u> is:

What in the world is "easy" after that passive participle, "made"? Probably some kind of retained objective complement??

If you have been able to understand and master this book, you are now ready to FIGURE OUT FOR YOURSELF an explanation for whatever you run into.

Find a good dictionary (and don't ask me what <u>that</u> is) and the oldest grammar book that you can get. Then dare the world to find a sentence that can stop you!

P.S. WAS it "made easy"? I tried.

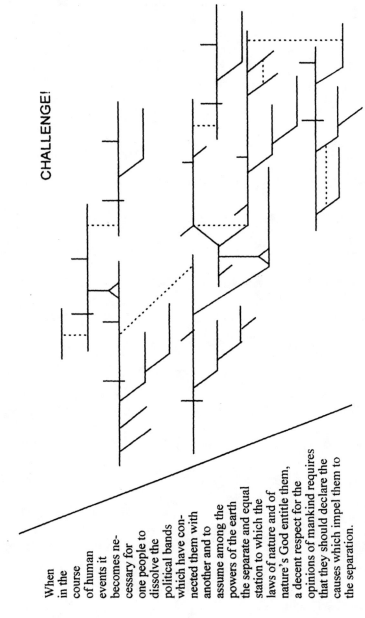

CHALLENGE!

When
in the
course
of human
events it
becomes ne-
cessary for
one people to
dissolve the
political bands
which have con-
nected them with
another and to
assume among the
powers of the earth
the separate and equal
station to which the
laws of nature and of
nature's God entitle them,
a decent respect for the
opinions of mankind requires
that they should declare the
causes which impel them to
the separation.

("The's" are omitted in
frame provided.)

APPENDIX

These pages contain an EXTREMELY CONDENSED summary of the traditional approach to sentence analysis and diagramming. It may be helpful as:

1) a quick review of "grammar" as a whole

2) an overview of an area to be studied

3) a handy source of answers to specific questions

4) a place to see where newly-learned material fits into the total picture.

MRS. D'S E-Z GUIDE TO GRAMMAR

I. PARTS OF SPEECH

The part of speech of a word depends on its use in the sentence.

NOUN—names a person, place, thing, idea.
> Mary sings. I went to Texas. See the box. He showed indifference.

PRONOUN—takes place of a noun.
> He sings. Everyone was tired. Give them time.
> I know whom you mean.

VERB—a word of action or being.
> Bill ran fast. He was happy. The rug faded. He wanted money.
> Paula has been singing. She might have seen me. I could try it.
> (Helping verbs: may   can   must   might   shall   will   should
> would   could   have   do   be.)

ADJECTIVE— modifies noun or pronoun.
> The big tree, Mother's ring, a kind person, sixteen blackbirds.
> ANSWERS the QUESTIONS: WHICH ONE?   WHAT   KIND?
> WHOSE?   HOW MANY?

ADVERB— modifies verb, adjective, or other adverb.
> Ran swiftly,   too fat,   very simply done,   stated clearly.
> ANSWERS the QUESTIONS: WHERE?   WHEN?   WHY?
> HOW?

CONJUNCTION—joins two words, phrases, or clauses.
> Bob and I;   down the street and around the corner;   While it
> snowed, the cat slept.

PREPOSITION—connects a noun or pronoun with rest of sentence and gives
> some relationship, such as space (in the box),   time (after
> school),   direction (toward the house),   cause (for his country.)

INTERJECTION—exclamation.
> Oh! Look at that!   Wow! He did it!
> Alas! We shall not meet again.

II. PHRASES

A phrase is a group of related words, without a subject and a verb, used as a single part of speech.

A. VERB PHRASE (NOT verbal phrase)—a verb and its helpers: he <u>might be sleeping</u>; she <u>should have been knitting</u>; they <u>did seem</u> angry.

B. PREPOSITIONAL PHRASE—preposition plus object (noun or pronoun) and any modifiers of the object.
    1. Adjective—The book <u>on the desk</u> is mine.
          (Tells which one.)
    2. Adverb—He put the pen <u>in his pocket</u>.
          (Tells where.)

C. VERBAL PHRASE—A verbal is a verb form used as another part of speech. There are three kinds of verbals.
    1. Participle (Adjective)—The <u>crying</u> child; (tells what kind). The book <u>sent</u> to him by Mary; (tells which one.)
    2. Gerund (Noun)—ALWAYS ends in –ing. I like <u>fishing</u>. He won by <u>trying</u> hard.
    3. Infinitive (Noun)—<u>To swim</u> is fun.
          (Adjective)—He is the one <u>to see</u>.
          (Adverb)—He came <u>to see</u> me.

Verbal phrases may have completers, modifiers, and sometimes "subjects."

III. CLAUSES

A clause is a group of words with a subject and a verb.

CLAUSES			
Main or Independent	Subordinate or Dependent		
	Noun	Adjective	Adverb
C A N S T A N D A L O N E (I see.)	Used as: Subj. P.N. D.O. Obj. Prep. I.O. Appos. (I know that I see.)	Modifies: Noun or Pronoun Introduced by Rel. Pro. (who, whose, whom, that, which) (The cat that I see is fat.)	Modifies: Verb, Adj., or Adv. Introduced by Subordinating Conjunction (I believe because I see.)

IV. KINDS OF VERBS

TRANSITIVE ACTIVE—ALWAYS carries action from Subject (Doer) to Direct Object (Receiver).

```
            TA        DO
   Bill | kicked |   cat
        |
```

TRANSITIVE PASSIVE—Carries action to Subject (Receiver).

```
              TP
   Cat | was kicked            (always has helping
       |                        verb and past participle.)
```

INTRANSITIVE COMPLETE—Subject is doer of action; no completer necessary.

```
                        IC
            Birds  |   sing
                   |
```

INTRANSITIVE LINKING—"State of being" verbs; act as "equals mark"; need predicate noun or predicate adjective to complete them.

```
            IL      PA                        IL       PN
  he    |   is   \  happy         he    |  became \   king
        |                               |
```

Linking Verbs:		Parts of "to be":	
be	sound	am	were
become	taste	are	being
seem	smell	is	been
appear	remain	was	
look	grow		
feel	stay		

V. SENTENCES BY STRUCTURE

SIMPLE SENTENCE—1 main clause.

COMPOUND SENTENCE—2 or more main clauses

COMPLEX SENTENCE—1 main, 1 or more dependent clauses

COMPOUND-COMPLEX SENTENCE—2 or more main, 1 or more dependent clauses.

DIAGRAMMING FORMS

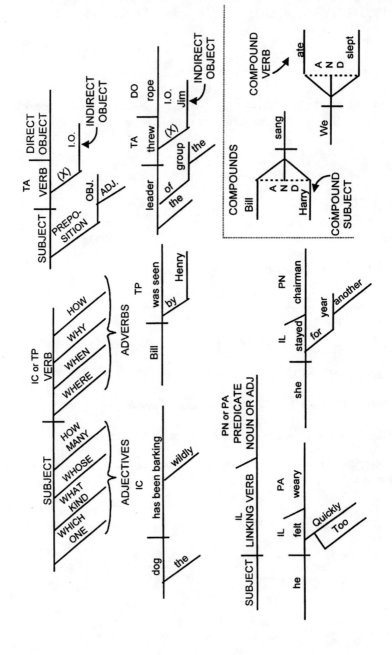

DIAGRAMMING FORMS

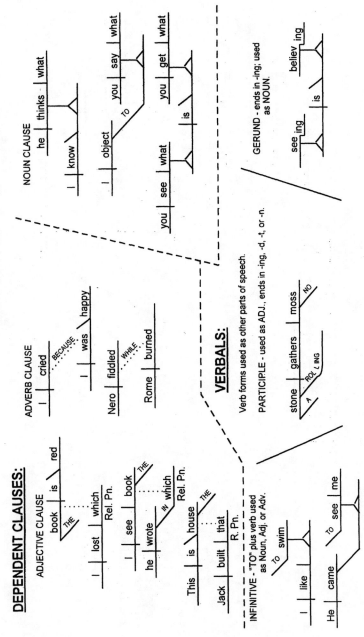

DEPENDENT CLAUSES:

ADJECTIVE CLAUSE

ADVERB CLAUSE

NOUN CLAUSE

INFINITIVE - "TO" plus verb used as Noun, Adj. or Adv.

VERBALS:

Verb forms used as other parts of speech.

PARTICIPLE - used as ADJ., ends in -ing, -d, -t, or -n.

GERUND - ends in -ing; used as NOUN.

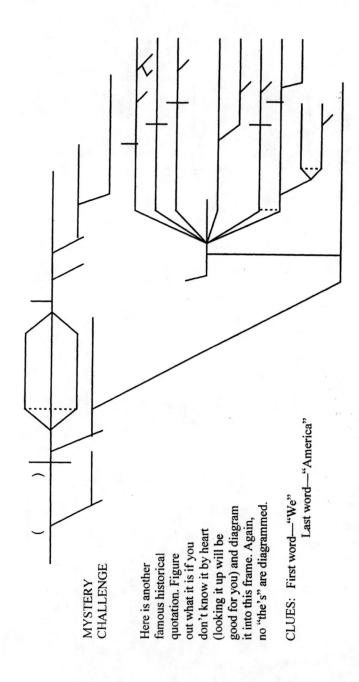

MYSTERY
CHALLENGE

Here is another
famous historical
quotation. Figure
out what it is if you
don't know it by heart
(looking it up will be
good for you) and diagram
it into this frame. Again,
no "the's" are diagrammed.

CLUES: First word—"We"

Last word—"America"

ANSWERS

ANSWERS

CHAPTER ONE

1-1 NOUNS
1. cat, fence, Siamese, window
2. Rex, slipper, father, tongue
3. birthday, Tuesday, peace, quiet, friends, vacation
4. Medicine Hat, Nebraska, Boston, culture, home, Harry

1-2 PRONOUNS
1. He, me, who, my, it, it
2. Somebody, something, one, it
3. Who, this, us
4. Those, you, what, these
5. Whose, I, I, him, everything, I, him

1-3 VERBS
1. competed, was interested
2. has been coming, has increased
3. might have been, upset, had left
4. has been snowing (**really** is an adverb), went

1-4 ADJECTIVES
1. Three, fat, red, their (possessive pronouns are also adjectives when they answer "whose"), our, telephone
2. The, only, (**to make** is an infinitive used as an adjective), a, good, chocolate, vanilla, strawberry, maple, chopped, marshmallow
3. an, enormous, Sunday, the, old, the, vine-covered, the, creaking, his, regular, Sunday
(Did you notice that some of these ADJECTIVES can also be NOUNS in other sentences?)

1-5 ADVERBS
1. Suddenly, very, wildly, hurriedly
2. (**When** is a conjunction introducing an adverb clause), thoroughly, very, carefully, well
3. gloomily, fully, soon, enough
4. never, again, so, very, eagerly

1-6 PREPOSITIONAL PHRASES

	Prepositions	Adjectives	Objects (Nouns)
1.	in		spring
	for		signs
	of	new	life
	in	our	yard
2.	after		school
	to	the	store
	for	a	way

(to spend is an INFINITIVE, not a preposition)

	for	his	birthday
3.	during	this	wave
		terrible	
		suffocating	
		heat	
	out of	his	house

(out of is considered one preposition)

4.	to	his	credit
	about	the	robbery
5.	in	the	dark
	of	the	night
	to		children
	under	my	bed

CHAPTER TWO

2-1

1. Rex | whined

2. Rex | was panting

3. Rex | might have been scratching

4. Rex | did bark

5. Rex | should have howled

6.   _Rex_ | _could have been growling_

7.   _Rex_ | _must have run_   8. _Rex_ | _had slept_

9.   _Rex_ | _may be eating_

10.   Rex | will have been digging

2-2 Subject <u>verb</u>
1. **Joe** <u>has been</u> here.
2. **You** <u>would have done</u> that.
3. **He** <u>did leave</u> why.
4. **You** <u>have been</u> where all day.
5. **He** <u>can mean</u> what by that statement.
6. **Who** <u>came</u> to the door? (No change necessary.)
7. **Mary** <u>could be</u> the one we want.
8. **Alex** <u>must</u> always <u>be driving</u> his car.
9. **He** <u>did pick</u> which one.
10. A poor **girl** <u>can trust</u> whom.

2-3

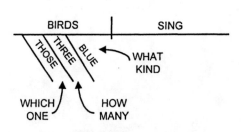

2-4

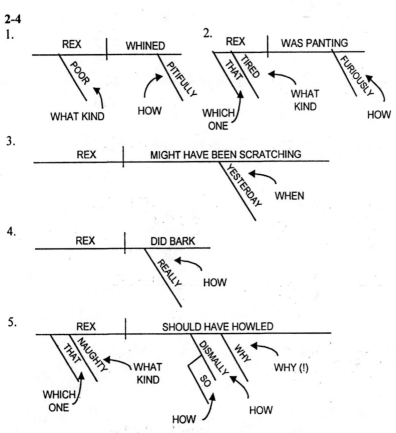

1. REX | WHINED — POOR / WHAT KIND, PITIFULLY / HOW

2. REX | WAS PANTING — THAT / TIRED / WHICH ONE, WHAT KIND / HOW, FURIOUSLY / HOW

3. REX | MIGHT HAVE BEEN SCRATCHING — YESTERDAY / WHEN

4. REX | DID BARK — REALLY / HOW

5. REX | SHOULD HAVE HOWLED — THAT / NAUGHTY / WHICH ONE, WHAT KIND / DISMALLY / SO / HOW, WHY / WHY (!) / HOW

From here on answers will be abbreviated. I hope you will not have trouble figuring out that "h b list" = "has been listening."

2-5

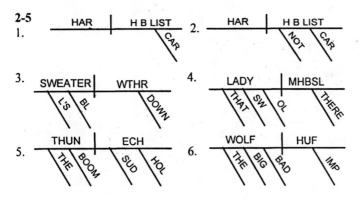

1. HAR | H B LIST — CAR

2. HAR | H B LIST — NOT / CAR

3. SWEATER | WTHR — L'S / BL, DOWN

4. LADY | MHBSL — THAT / SW / OL, THERE

5. THUN | ECH — THE / BOOM, SUD / HOL

6. WOLF | HUF — THE / BIG / BAD, IMP

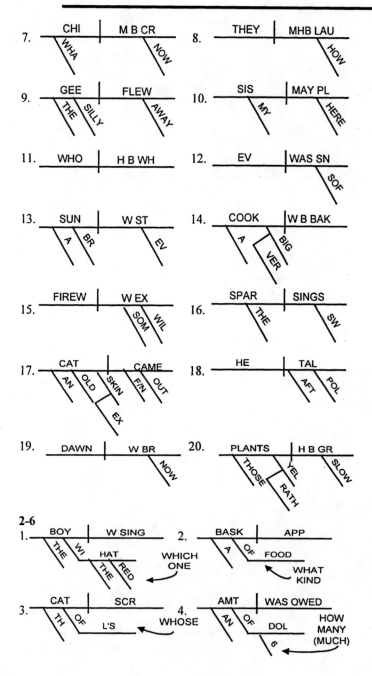

7. CHI | M B CR WHA NOW

8. THEY | MHB LAU HOW

9. GEE | FLEW THE SILLY AWAY

10. SIS | MAY PL MY HERE

11. WHO | H B WH

12. EV | WAS SN SOF

13. SUN | W ST A BR EV

14. COOK | W B BAK A BIG VER

15. FIREW | W EX SOM WIL

16. SPAR | SINGS THE SW

17. CAT | CAME AN OLD SKIN F/N OUT EX

18. HE | TAL AFT POL

19. DAWN | W BR NOW

20. PLANTS | H B GR THOSE YEL RATH SLOW

2-6

1. BOY | W SING THE WI HAT THE RED WHICH ONE

2. BASK | APP A OF FOOD WHAT KIND

3. CAT | SCR TH OF L'S WHOSE

4. AMT | WAS OWED AN OF DOL HOW MANY (MUCH) 6

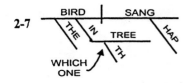

2-7

2-8

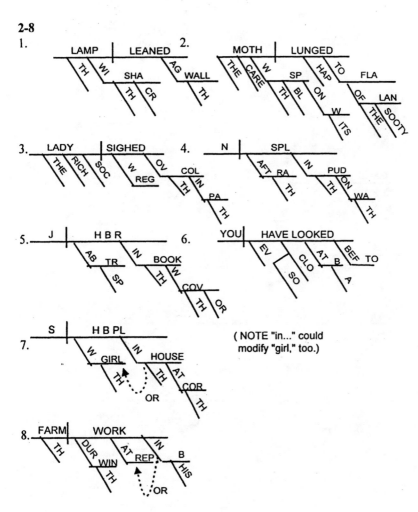

(NOTE "in..." could modify "girl," too.)

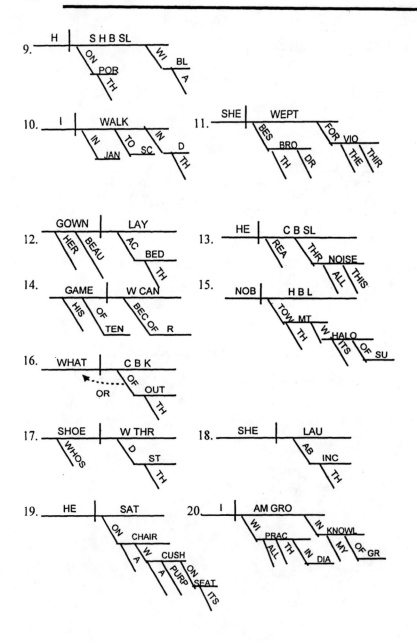

2-9

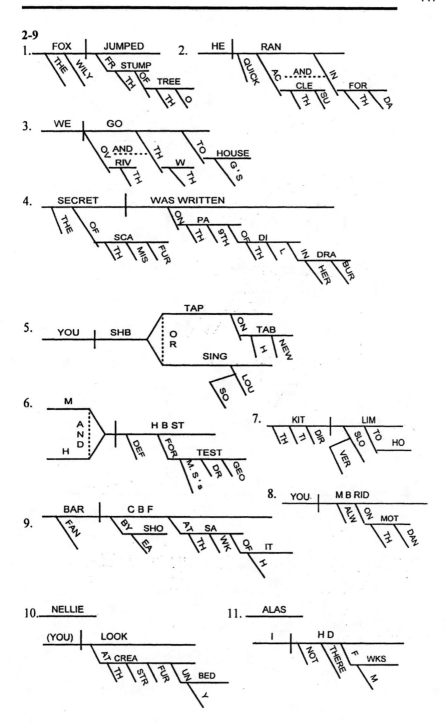

12. NEL
13.
14. HAH
15.

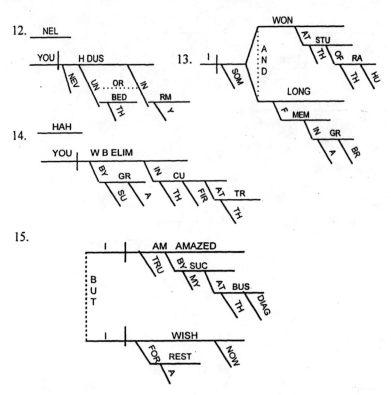

CHAPTER THREE

3-1

1. N | TA (PUT) | DO D ... IN SINK TH

2. YOU | TA H S | DO (COLLAR) ... TH CAT'S

3. (WAITERS) | TA Q | DO JOBS ... ALL TH ON F TH

4. I | TA DO BEL | DO (STORIES) ... NOT TH

5. OTTO | TA (THREW) | DO FOOD ... TO SQ TH

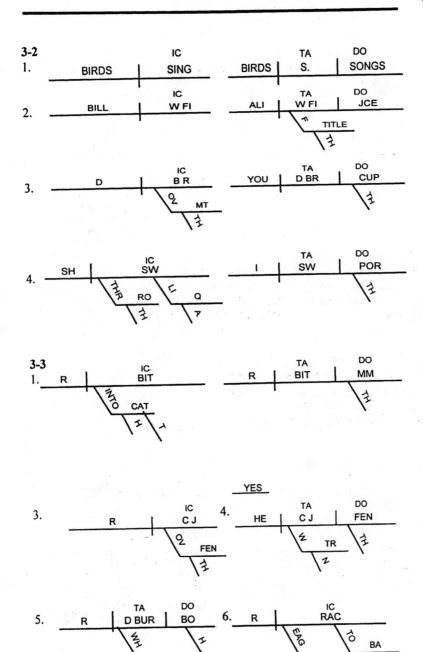

3-2

1. BIRDS | SING (IC) — BIRDS | S. (TA) | SONGS (DO)

2. BILL | W FI (IC) — ALI | W FI (TA) | JCE (DO) / TITLE / TH

3. D | B R (IC) / OV / MT / TH — YOU | D BR (TA) | CUP (DO) / TH

4. SH | SW (IC) / THR / RO / TH / LI / Q / A — I | SW (TA) | POR (DO) / TH

3-3

1. R | BIT (IC) / INTO / CAT / H / T — R | BIT (TA) | MM (DO) / TH

3. R | C J (IC) / OV / FEN / TH

4. YES — HE | C J (TA) | FEN (DO) / W / TR / N / TH

5. R | D BUR (TA) | BO (DO) / WH / H

6. R | RAC (IC) / EAG / TO / BA / TH

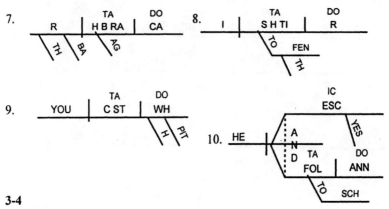

3-4

1. The ball was lost by Harry.
2. The antique safe was broken by the force of the blow.
3. The tinkle of breaking glass was heard by everyone in the room.
4. A good time was had by all the people.
5. With the arrival of Harry, the rehearsal was begun by us.

3-5

1. The shutter hit Dorothy on the head.
2. (We) have often seen Melinda at the opera.
3. In some countries chaperones guard girls.
4. A spider might have bitten George.
5. Mother, (I) smashed your favorite lamp.

3-6

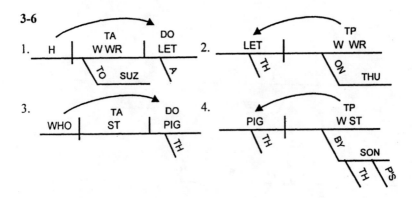

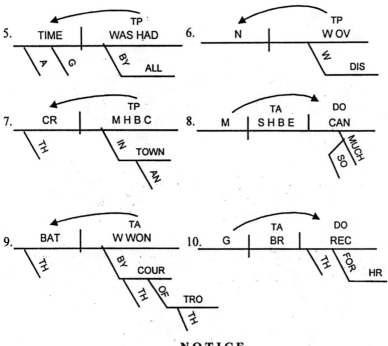

5. TIME | WAS HAD — TP — A G BY ALL

6. N | W OV — TP — W DIS

7. CR | MHBC — TP — TH IN TOWN AN

8. M | SHBE | CAN — TA — DO — SO MUCH

9. BAT | W WON — TA — TH BY COUR TH OF TRO TH

10. G | BR | REC — TA — DO — TH FOR HR

NOTICE
From this point on, ANSWERS will OMIT
"THE's."

3-7

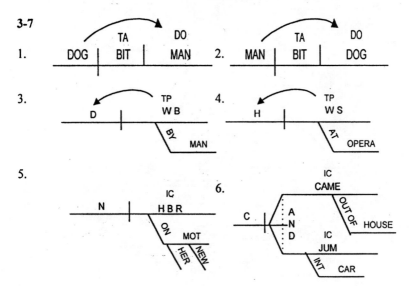

1. DOG | BIT | MAN — TA — DO

2. MAN | BIT | DOG — TA — DO

3. D | WB — TP — BY MAN

4. H | WS — TP — AT OPERA

5. N | HBR — IC — ON MOT HER NEW

6. C | CAME / JUM — IC — A N D OUT OF HOUSE — INT CAR

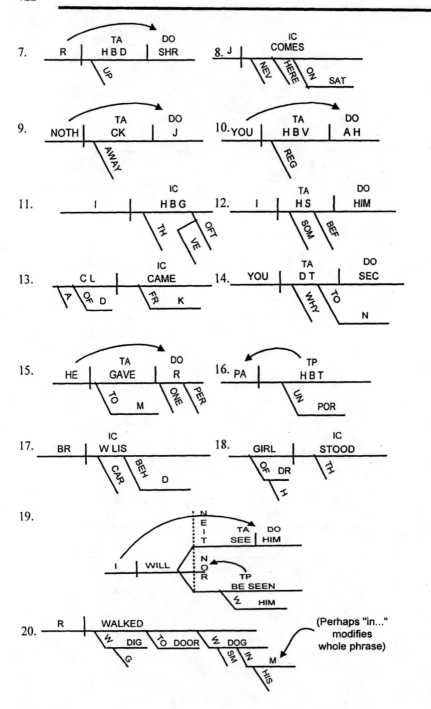

7. R | HBD | SHR — TA DO — UP

8. J | COMES IC — NEV / HERE / ON SAT

9. NOTH | CK | J — TA DO — AWAY

10. YOU | HBV | AH — TA DO — REG

11. I | HBG IC — TH / VE / OFT

12. I | HS | HIM — TA DO — SOM / BEF

13. CL | CAME IC — A / OF D — FR K

14. YOU | DT | SEC — TA DO — WHY / TO / N

15. HE | GAVE | R — TA DO — TO M / ONE PER

16. PA | HBT TP — UN / POR

17. BR | WLIS IC — CAR / BEH D

18. GIRL | STOOD IC — OF DR / H — TH

19. I | WILL — NEIT — TA DO — SEE | HIM — NOR — TP — BE SEEN — HIM

20. R | WALKED — W / DIG / G — TO DOOR — W DOG — SM IN M — HIS

(Perhaps "in..." modifies whole phrase)

3-8

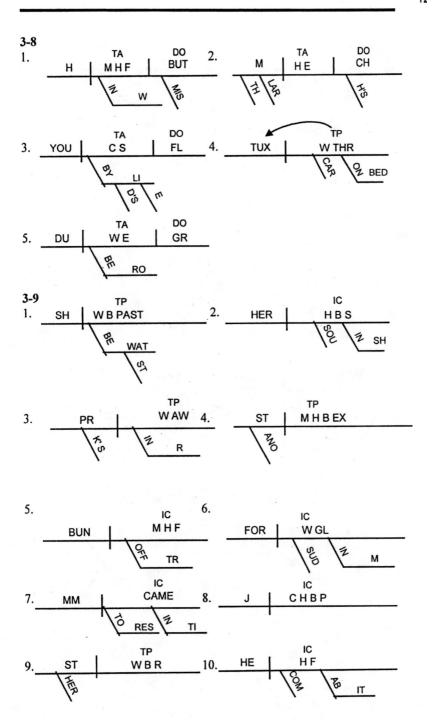

1.
   - H | TA MHF | DO BUT
   - IN W
   - MIS

2.
   - M | TA HE | DO CH
   - TH LAR
   - H'S

3.
   - YOU | TA CS | DO FL
   - BY LI
   - D'S E

4.
   - TUX | TP WTHR
   - CAR
   - ON BED

5.
   - DU | TA WE | DO GR
   - BE RO

3-9

1.
   - SH | TP WB PAST
   - BE WAT
   - ST

2.
   - HER | IC HBS
   - SOU
   - IN SH

3.
   - PR | TP WAW
   - K'S
   - IN R

4.
   - ST | TP MHBEX
   - ANO

5.
   - BUN | IC MHF
   - OFF TR

6.
   - FOR | IC WGL
   - SUD
   - IN M

7.
   - MM | IC CAME
   - TO RES
   - IN TI

8.
   - J | IC CHBP

9.
   - ST | TP WBR
   - HER

10.
   - HE | IC HF
   - COM
   - AB IT

3-10

1.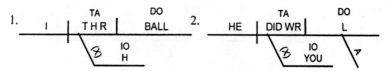

2.

3. By November I had mailed Vernon a present.

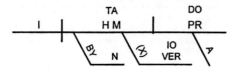

4. He had saved Ann a seat in the front row.

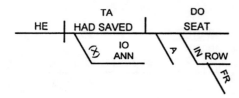

5. Lottie gives Mervin a pain.   6. Throw me a rope!

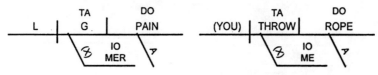

7. Have you baked the class a cake?   8. Zelda did knit him a sweater.

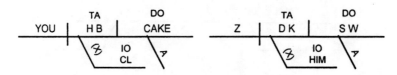

3-11

IL

IS, WAS, HAS BEEN, ETC.

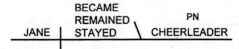
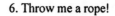

3-12

1. SH | H B L \ IL PA SICK   2. I | AM BE \ IL PA ANGR
   LAT   BY MIN

3. TR | D L \ IL PA BLUE   4. N A / AND / H D \ SO IL \ UNH PA AF G
   IN BRM

5. C | M H B \ IL PA FR   6. L | C H A \ IL PA BL
   TH YES   BEF TH

7. MAN | H R \ IL PN PR   8. H | IS \ IL PN PR
   TH OL FOR Y CL'S OUR   IN E NS A

9. AC | SE \ IL PA Y   10. H | SB \ IL PA WIN
   B U T AT FIR   AL OF R EV
   GR IL PA OL
   DUR PL

3-13

1. BEG | LO IC   2. HE | APP IC
   IN W   SUD AT DOR

3. R | SM TA | STR DO   4. FI | SOU TA | AL DO

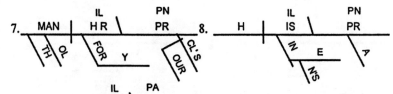
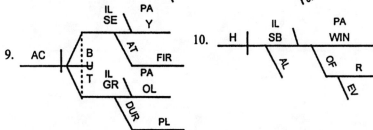

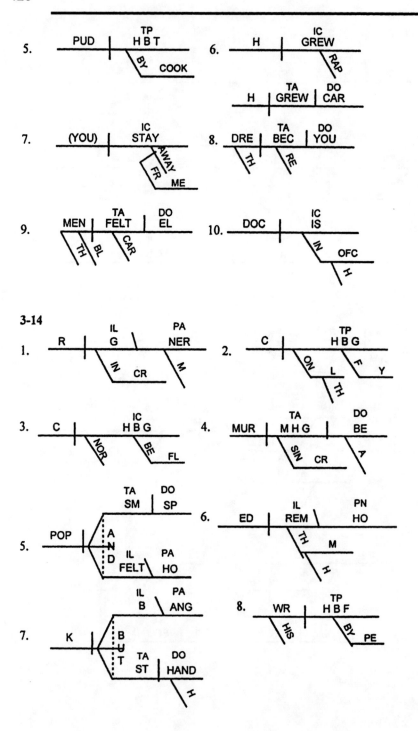

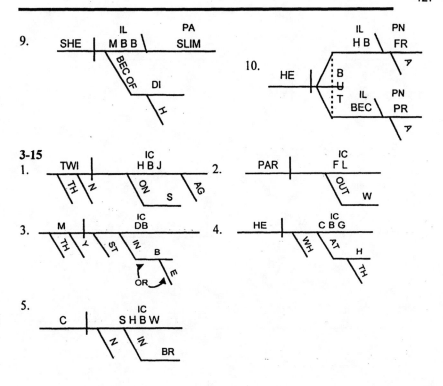

9. SHE | M B B (IL) \ SLIM (PA) / BEC OF \ DI / H

10. HE | H B (IL) \ FR (PN) ... B U T ... BEC (IL) \ PR (PN)

3-15

1. TWI | H B J (IC) \ TH \ N \ ON \ S \ AG

2. PAR | F L (IC) \ OUT \ W

3. M | DB (IC) \ TH \ Y \ ST \ IN \ B OR E

4. HE | C B G (IC) \ WH \ AT \ H \ TH

5. C | S H B W (IC) \ N \ IN \ BR

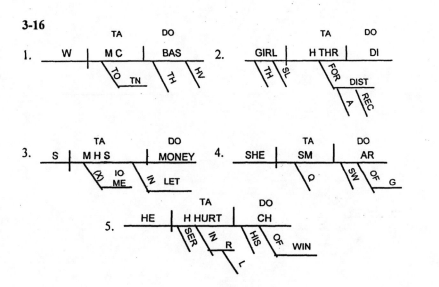

3-16

1. W | M C (TA) | BAS (DO) \ TO TN \ TH \ HV

2. GIRL | H THR (TA) | DI (DO) \ TH \ SL \ FOR \ DIST \ REC \ A

3. S | M H S (TA) | MONEY (DO) \ IO ME \ IN LET

4. SHE | SM (TA) | AR (DO) \ O \ SW \ OF G

5. HE | H HURT (TA) | CH (DO) \ SER \ IN R \ HIS \ OF WIN \ L

3-17

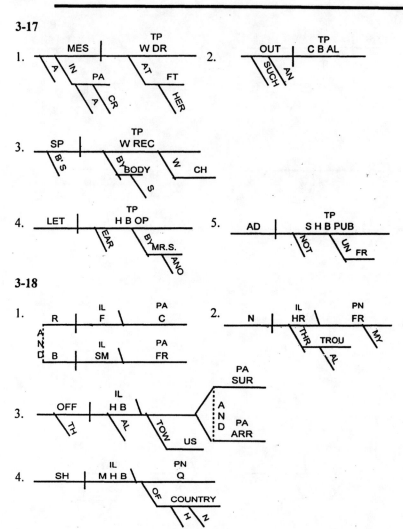

3-18

3-19

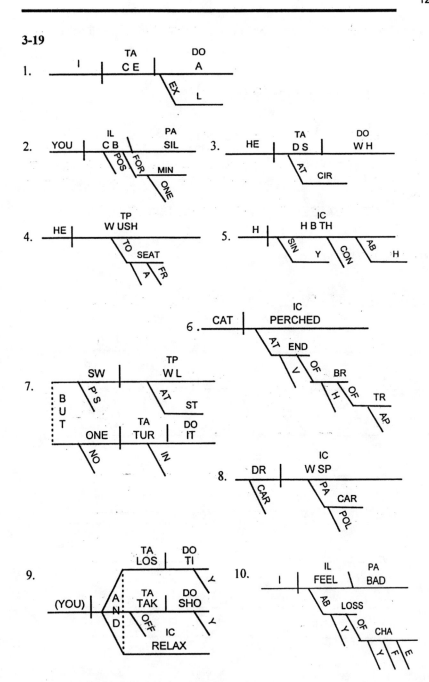

From here on, verbs and complements will not be labeled. You will be expected to know that:

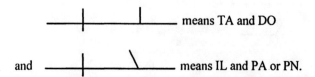

means TA and DO

and ⎯⎯⎯⎯⎯⎯ means IL and PA or PN.

The only other tricky thing is whether an uncomplemented verb is IC or TP. But most of the time it is not necessary to show that difference, just so you understand it.

BUT PLEASE DON'T FORGET THESE DISTINCTIONS!

CHAPTER FOUR

4-1

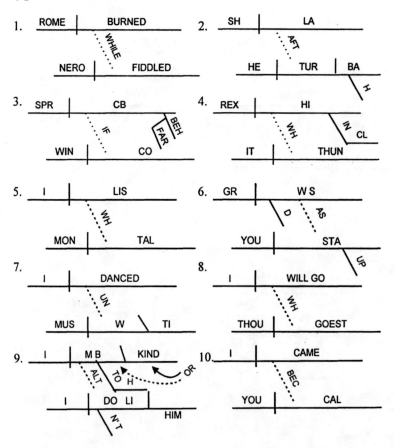

4-2

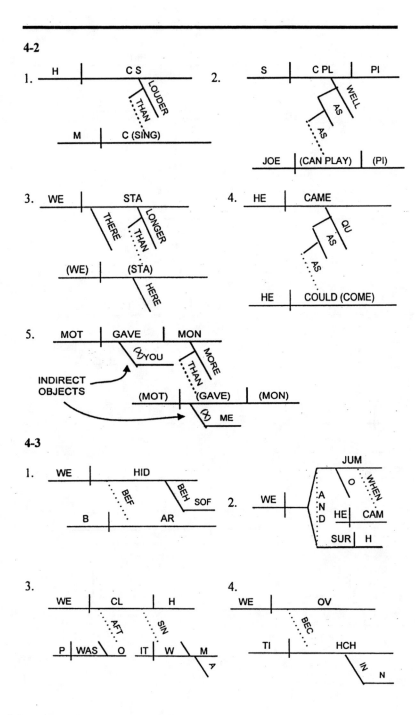

4-3

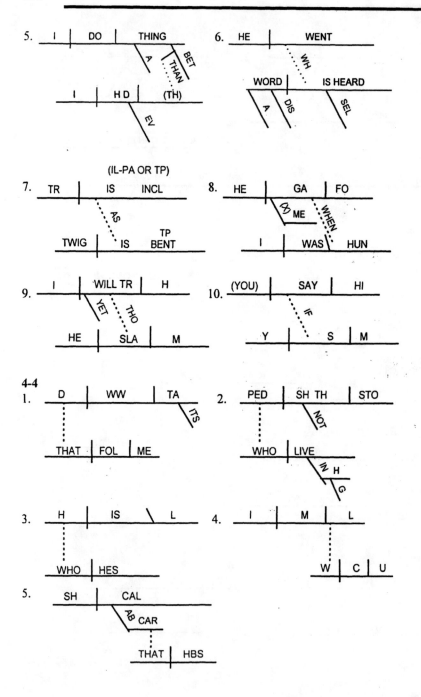

4-5

1.

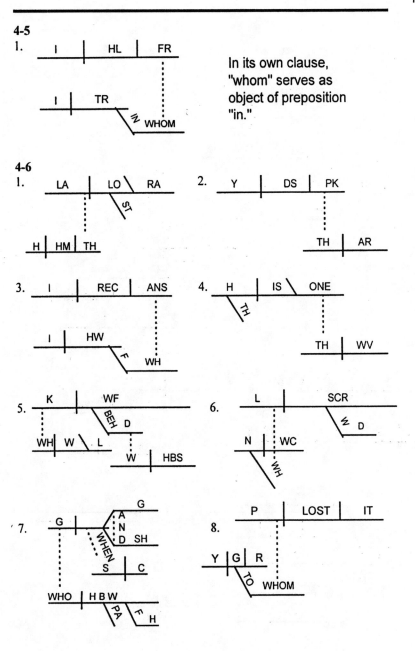

In its own clause, "whom" serves as object of preposition "in."

4-6

9.

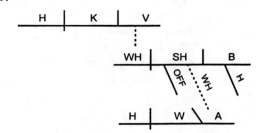

10.

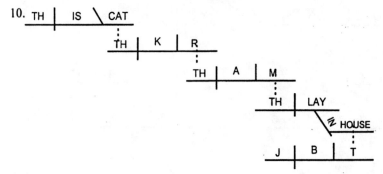

4-7

1.

2.

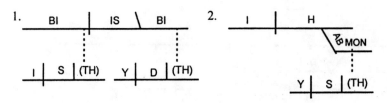

3.

4.

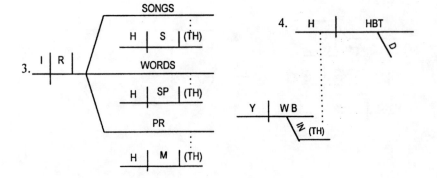

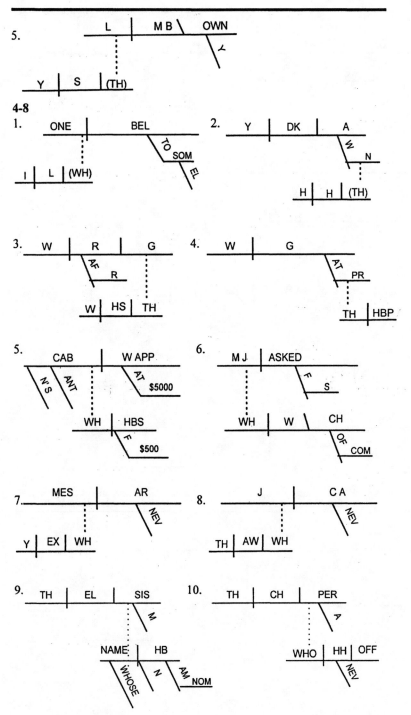

5.

4-8

1.

2.

3.

4.

5.

6.

7.

8.

9.

10.

4-9

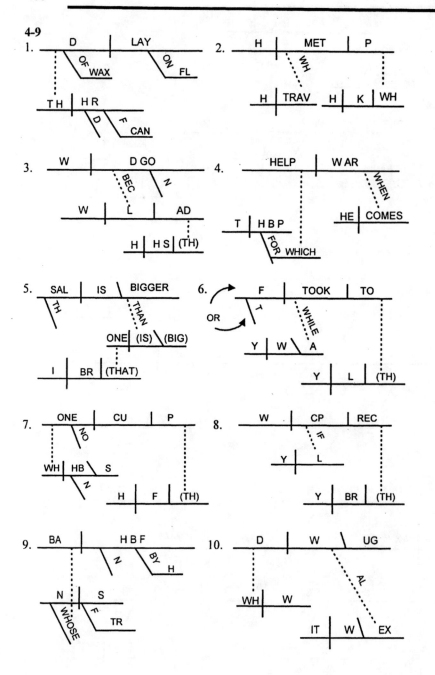

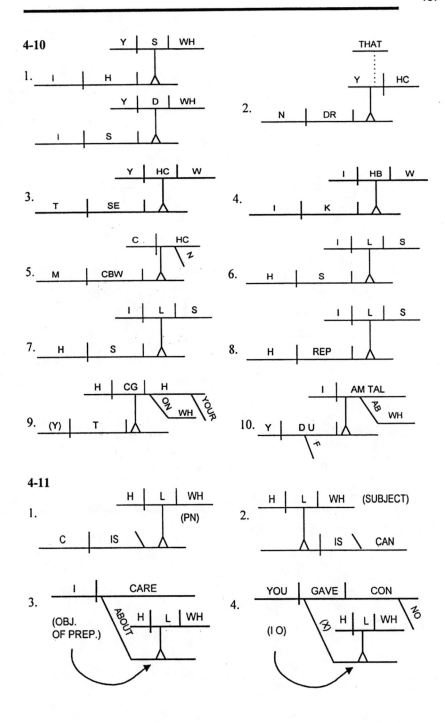

4-12

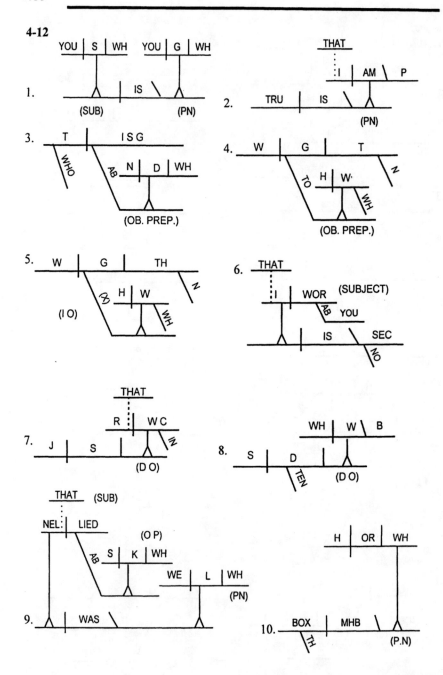

4-13

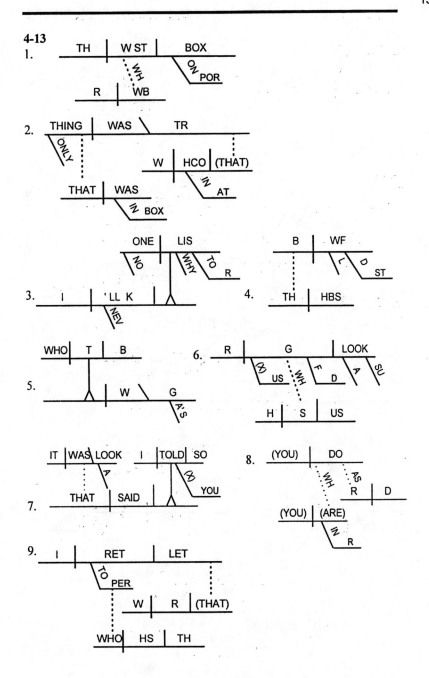

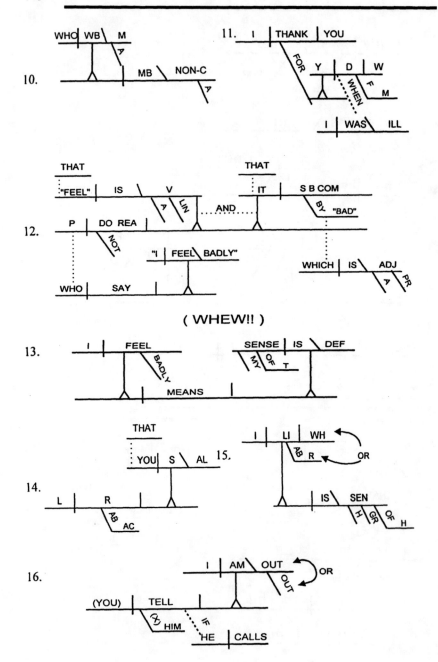

(WHEW!!)

17.

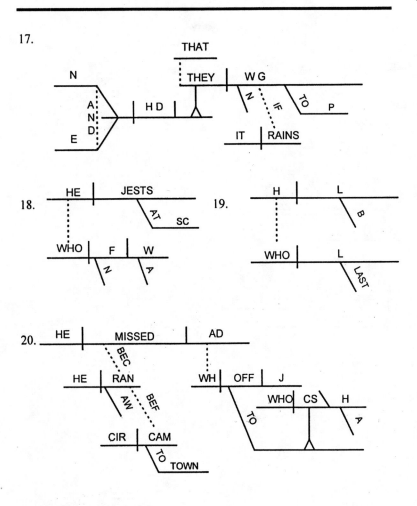

18.

19.

20.

CHAPTER FIVE

5-1

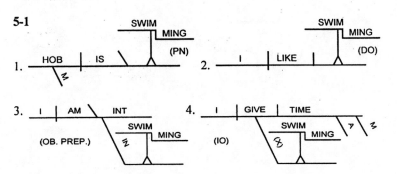

5-2

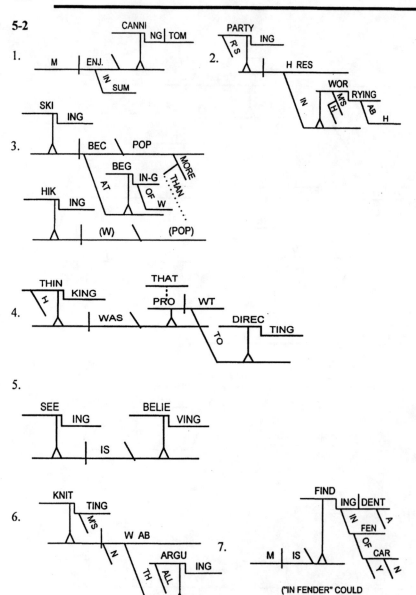

("IN FENDER" COULD
ALSO MODIFY "DENT")

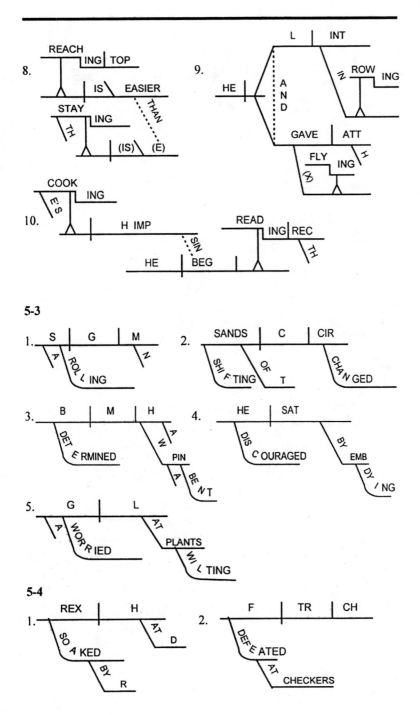

8.

9.

10.

5-3

1.

2.

3.

4.

5.

5-4

1.

2.

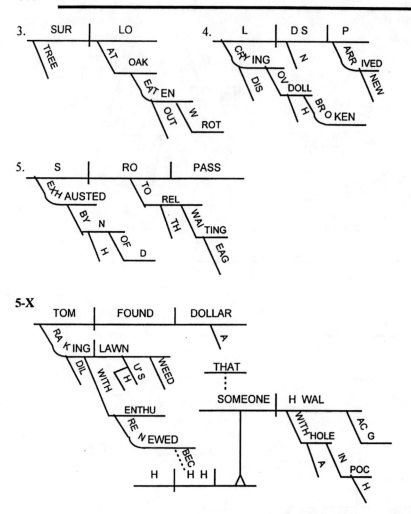

"Because" clause could also modify "raking" or the whole prepositional phrase, "with, etc." (A well-written sentence would not have these ambiguities, but wasn't it fun to do?)

5-5

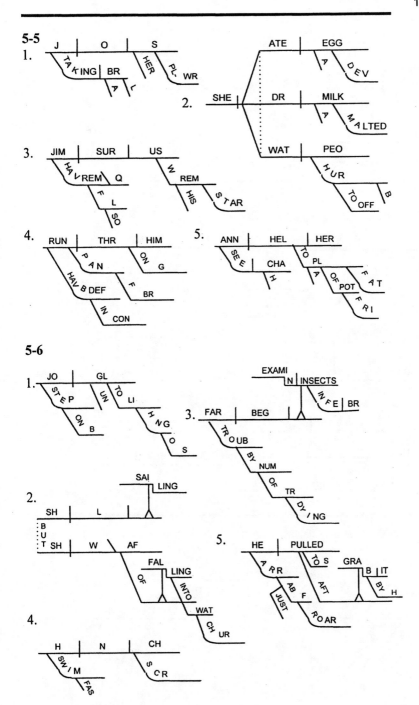

5-6

5-7

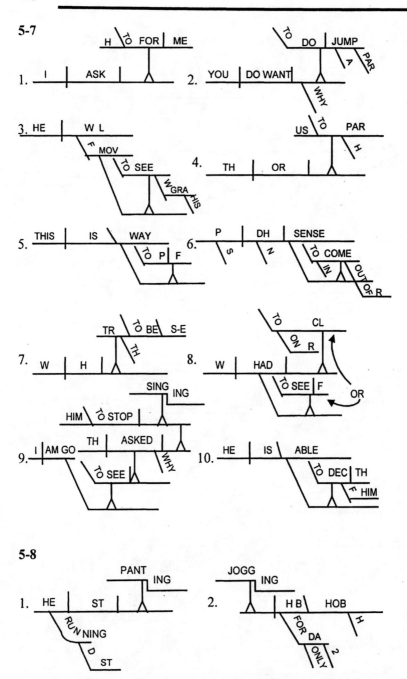

5-8

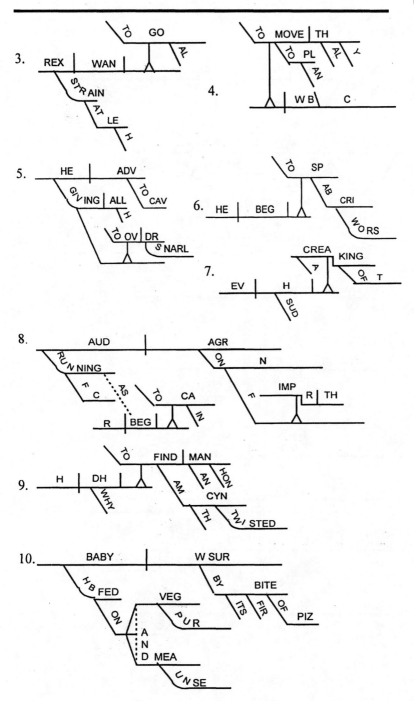

CHAPTER SIX

6-1

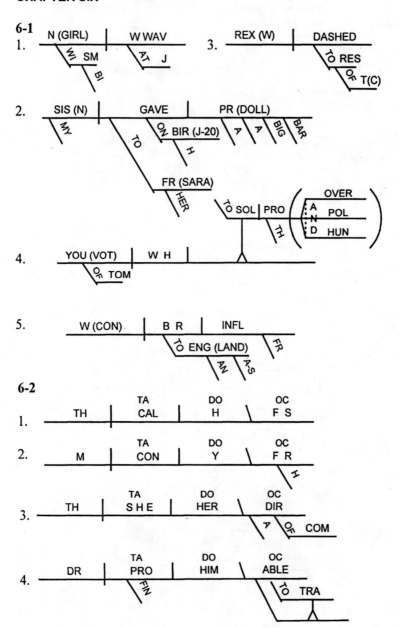

5.

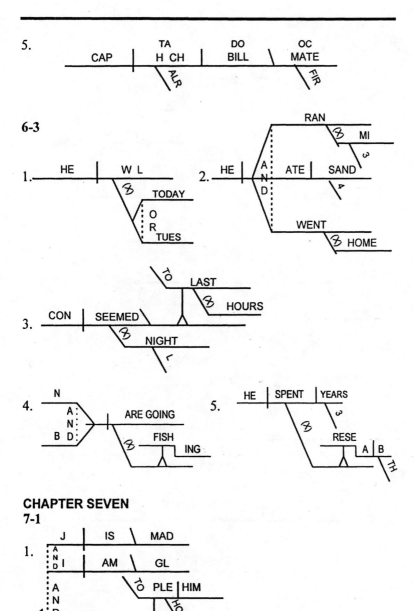

6-3

1.

2.

3.

4.

5.

CHAPTER SEVEN
7-1

1.

(COMPOUND)

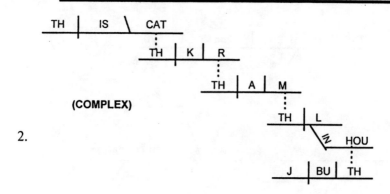

(COMPLEX)

2.

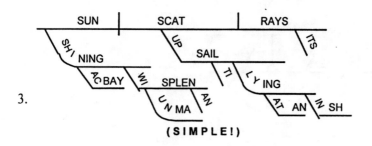

(SIMPLE!)

3.

4.

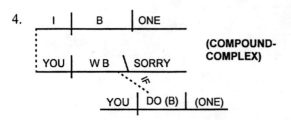

(COMPOUND-COMPLEX)

5.

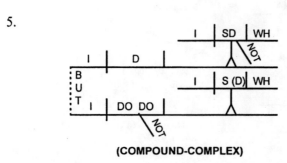

(COMPOUND-COMPLEX)

INDEX

A

Active voice. *See* verb
Adjective, 9, 14-17
  clause, 53-60, 89
  predicate, 27, 40-41
  questions, 9, 14, 17
Adverb, 9-10, 14-17
  clause, 47-53, 90-92
  conjunctive, 10
  noun used as, 82-85, 97
  questions, 9, 14, 17
Answers, 110-151
Antecedent, 59
Appositive, 80-81
Articles, 9, 15

B

Be, parts of, 13, 44
  followed by prepositional phrase, 96

C

Case
  nominative, 93-94
  objective, 93-95, 77
  personal pronoun, 92-95
  possessive, 69
  subject of gerund, 69
  subject of infinitive, 77
  who, whom, 55, 56
Clause, 18, 46, 104
  adjective, 53-60, 89
  adverb, 90-92, 48-53
  dependent or subordinate, 46-48, 53, 60
  elliptical, 50-52
  main or independent, 46-48
  noun, 60-64
  restrictive and non-restrictive, 59
Commas
  after introductory participial phrase, 72
  with appositives, 81
  with non-restrictive clauses, 59
Complement, 40
  objective complement, 81-82
Compound
  -complex sentence, 87-88
  elements, 22-23
  sentences, 23, 87
Conjunction, 10
  coordinating, 10, 22, 50
  subordinating, 10, 49-50, 90-91

D

Determiner, 8
Diagramming forms summarized, 106-107
Direct address, 24

G

Gerund, 67-70

I

Infinitive, 31, 76-78
  without "to," 78
Interjection, 11, 24
Intransitive. *See* verb.
Introductory word, 25

L

Like and as, 90-91
Linking verbs, list of, 27

M

Modifiers, 14-16
Mood, 91-92

N

Nominative. *See* case.
Nominative absolute, 74

Non-restrictive clauses, 59
Noun, 7-8, 97
  abstract, 7
  adverbial, 82-85, 97
  as adjective, 97
  clause, 60-64
  common, 7
  concrete, 7
  jobs, 60, 80
  predicate, 27, 40-41
  proper, 7

O
Object
  direct, 27, 30, 60-61
  indirect, 37-38, 64
  of preposition, 18, 64
  retained, 38

P
Participle, 70-75
  dangling, 72-73
Parts of speech, 7, 102,
Passive voice. *See* verb.
Phrase, 18, 46, 103
Predicate, 12
  adjective; noun, 27, 40-41
  nominative, 62-63
Prepositions and prepositional phrases, 6,
    11, 18-21, 46, 47, 64, 95-96, 103
Pronoun, 8, 92-95
  in noun clauses, 61
  missing relative, 58
  personal, 93-95
  relative, 53-58

Q
Questions, how to analyze, 13-14

S
Sentence, 4, 15, 46
  classified by structure, 87-88, 105
  definition, 4
  simple, 87
Subject, 12
  noun clause as, 63
  of gerund, 69-70
  of infinitive, 77
Subordinating conjunction, 10, 49-50, 90-91

T
Than and as, 50-52
Transitive. *See* verb.

U
Understood "you," 23-24

V
Verb, 8-9, 27, 28-41, 104-105
  active voice, 27, 29, 35
  chart, 27
  helping, 8, 13, 74
  intransitive complete, 27, 28-29
  intransitive linking, 27, 39-42
  passive voice, 27, 32-33, 35
  transitive and intransitive, 27, 28, 30-31
Verbals, 67-78, 103
  gerund, 67-70
  infinitives, 76-78
  participles, 70-75
  phrase, 46, 69-70

W
"Where" and "when" as relative pronouns,
    89-90
"Which"
  as relative pronoun, 53
  indefinite, 89
Who, whom, whose, 53, 55-57

Printed in the United States
107875LV00001B/4/A